The Rise and Rise of the Private Art Museum

Hot Topics In The Art World

Published in association with Sotheby's Institute of Art

Series Editors

Jeffrey Boloten and Juliet Hacking, Sotheby's Institute of Art, London

This series of short, thought-provoking and sometimes controversial books debates key issues of current relevance to art-world professionals working in both the private and public sectors. The texts give wider visibility to some critical areas of professional art-world practice, considering what disruptors are challenging the status quo and how the art world is likely to be transformed over the next decades as a result.

International Series Advisory Board

The Rise and Rise of the Private Art Museum

Georgina Adam

LUND HUMPHRIES

Sotheby's INSTITUTE OF ART

First published in 2021 by Lund Humphries
in association with Sotheby's Institute of Art

Lund Humphries
Office 3, Book House
261A City Road
London EC1V 1JX
UK

www.lundhumphries.com

ISBN (hardback): 978-1-84822-384-4
ISBN (eBook PDF): 978-1-84822-385-1
ISBN (eBook ePub): 978-1-84822-386-8
ISBN (eBook Mobi): 978-1-84822-387-5

A Cataloguing-in-Publication record for this book is available from the British Library

Copy edited by Michela Parkin
Designed by Crow Books
Set in Caslon Pro and Sofia Pro
Printed in Estonia

Contents

Foreword

There has been a pronounced shift of power within the art market ecosystem in response to global financial pressures and the policies designed to deal with them. The ongoing contraction of cultural sector funding has seen museum acquisitions and operations budgets steadily compromised. Ever-increasing global art market prices have also undermined the ability of museums to renew and refresh their collections. With their inevitably strained resources, public museums often struggle to satisfy the substantial demands of the collector/patron communities on which their collections, and institutions, very much rely.

Against this backdrop, the very nature of art philanthropy has been steadily shifting. It is the collectors themselves who have been increasingly taking on the essential caretaking roles and responsibilities for cultural artefacts. With collectors increasingly keen to closely control the future legacy of their hard-won, and much cherished, art collections, they are increasingly turning to bespoke Private Museum solutions. In more newly developing regions, private patrons, and their museums, can harness enormous power to build and transform a city, region and even a nation's cultural landscape – providing the crucial cultural foundation that many governments cannot, or choose not to fund or support.

In *The Rise and Rise of the Private Art Museum*, Georgina Adam deploys her unparalleled art-world knowledge, analytical clarity, and scrupulous research to shine a light on this important paradigm shift of our times.

Jeffrey Boloten and Juliet Hacking, June 2021

Acknowledgements

On 11 February 2020 I was due to fly to China and Australia on a research trip for a book about private museums. That trip never happened for obvious reasons and, although I had already visited over 50 of these institutions, my plan to see many more was curtailed by the pandemic.

As a result, I am so grateful to the many people who subsequently talked to me over Zoom or other platforms, as well as those I had already interviewed before the pandemic struck. My thanks go to Adrian Ellis, Alain Quemin, Alex Petalas, Anita Zabludowicz, Bomi Odofunade, Catherine Hickley, Charles Saumarez Smith, Diana Wierbicki, Doug Woodham, Elizabeth Ann Macgregor, Elizabeth Neilson, Gail Lord, Grace Ai, Gordon Elliott, Grażyna Kulczyk, Han Nefkens, Howard Rachofsky, James Carleton, Kenny Schachter, Laurent Le Bon, Lisa Movius, Sir Mark Jones, Marta Gnyp, Martin Bailey, Maxwell Anderson, Mera Rubell, Patrizia Sandretto Re Rebaudengo, Philip Dodd, Rajeeb and Nadia Samdani, Rebecca Wei, Sébastien Montabonel, Steven Kettle, Ziba Ardalan and others who wished to remain anonymous.

I also would like to thank the arts editor of the *Financial Times*, Jan Dalley, for originally suggesting this subject to me; Jane Morris and Tim Schneider for talking me through the initial framing, and the authors of three books – Georgina S. Walker; Cristina Bechtler, Dora Imhof and Chris Dercon; and András Szántó – for writing texts that were immensely helpful. I am not a museum specialist and this is an outsider's view of the subject; I hope it will be judged as such.

My thanks also go to my editor Lucy Myers of Lund Humphries for bearing with me, to Jeffrey Boloten and Juliet Hacking of Sotheby's Institute of Art for initiating this series, to Michela Parkin for exemplary copy editing and, as always, to the team at *The Art Newspaper* for their insights. Any errors are mine alone. My husband Christopher and my family continue, of course, to be the best support structure anyone could hope for.

Introduction

Private art museums have become a cultural, social and economic phenomenon of this century. They have proliferated geographically in the last two decades, with new ones being thrown up across the world as I write, from China and New Zealand to Argentina or Iceland.

The number of such museums is growing all the time and, while the 2020–21 global pandemic temporarily froze many projects, several new institutions are set to be opened after 2021. Some are more personal, such as the Srihatta – Samdani Art Centre and Sculpture Park being built in Sylhet, Bangladesh by Rajeeb and Nadia Samdani; some are huge, such as the vast corporate museum for the Fondation Cartier due in 2024 in Paris, France, or GES-2, an immense power station transformed by a Russian billionaire into an art space in Moscow, Russia. Or there is the small Longlati Foundation, lodged in the 'Art Tower' in West Bund, Shanghai, China; or the Kunsthalle Praha in Prague, Czech Republic, housed in a converted former power substation.

These institutions are the way deep-pocketed collectors give the public access to their art treasures or offer a platform for art and artists – sometimes in spectacular, architect-designed buildings, more occasionally in their own homes. They are a way of 'giving back to society' through educational and outreach programmes, bolstering the cultural credentials of the region, supporting local artists – and leaving the legacy of the founder's name and public-spiritedness for future generations.

They can revive a declining city or even a region (the 'Bilbao effect',[1] as seen in Hobart, Tasmania with the Museum of Old and New Art), foster new artistic practices with a nimbleness that more slow-footed, publicly funded institutions cannot always match and organise blockbuster exhibitions that public museums cannot always afford. They are also a way for large companies, notably in the luxury goods sector, to 'brand' themselves as not just profit-obsessed corporate behemoths but as progressive, socially committed entities offering something back to the community.

All this comes at a time when publicly funded museums are under unprecedented pressure on many fronts. (See Chapter 1 for a discussion of the definition of public and private museums). Their very role as storehouses of artefacts, their traditional mission of collecting, conserving, researching, explaining and displaying the objects of the past and present, are under unprecedented strains. These strains range from the ethics of sponsorship to accusations of racial injustice – both in staffing and in the works displayed – decolonisation issues and the environmental cost of the exhibitions they put on, involving as they do crating, handling and shipping works around the world. Indeed, the very definition of a museum today is contentious. Add to this the hammer blow of the 2020–21 pandemic, which left many museums teetering on the brink of financial wipe-out, as revenue from ticketing, shops, restaurants and gala events simply disappeared.

In addition, philanthropy has changed. It is much more impact-based than in the past; donors today are often looking for measurable outcomes when they decide where to put their charity dollars, euros or pounds. 'Philanthrocapitalism' – when donors apply the business techniques they honed in their professional lives to charitable giving – has made a major impact on how the rich choose to give money, and to what causes. These 'new philanthropists', writes Paul Vallely in his book *Philanthropy: From Aristotle to Zuckerberg*, are 'driven by the quirks and flukes of their own life story, personal experience, political conviction or business interests'.[2] And he continues by noting the shift from traditional philanthropy to philanthrocapitalism, reflected in the way wealth was acquired. In the past it was often inherited; today it is mostly self-made. Today's mega-rich want to do more than just write a cheque for a good cause; as successful entrepreneurs, they want to be more hands-on, and they often have the skills and acumen to do so.

But the problem is that philanthrocapitalism is an uneasy fit with culture, which has always struggled to prove its worth in a way that can be quantified. As the cultural consultant András Szántó notes: 'This has left us with, in a way, a more personally-driven, as it were connoisseur funder, who is supporting the arts not because of measurable impact or other foundation or policy priorities, but because they're simply passionate about art – and this is how they want to spend their money.'[3]

As a result, collectors are establishing their own spaces, to showcase their treasures, preserve the integrity of their collection and at the same time fulfil their philanthropic purposes. Their motivations are complex, as we shall see in Chapter 2. They vary from the laudable desire to share their good fortune with the public, to wanting to contribute to the cultural discourse of the age and improve the cultural offer of their city or region. But there is also distrust of public institutions, and in some cases more problematic aims: self-aggrandisement, hyping the value of their collection, getting better access to desirable art and getting whopping tax breaks. Indeed, one of my interviewees, a former museum director, dismissed private museums as merely 'tombs for trophies' and tax dodges for billionaires.[4]

The picture is far more complex, as we shall see in the following pages. Private museums give the public access to works of art they might otherwise never be able to see; fill the gap left by cash-strapped public institutions; supply educational programmes for the local community; and, in many countries, where the state cannot or will not fund contemporary art, provide a platform for local art and artists. And some accumulations will move into public ownership, just as many of the stellar collections of the 19th century also evolved into the great museums we see today.

At the same time, the current rise in the number and scale of private museums has created tension with the public sector. The colossal increase in wealth this century, and the resulting rise in the price of art, has hobbled publicly funded institutions. Billionaires have forced prices up by chasing the most desirable contemporary artists and the most sought-after historic artists, shutting out state institutions. And this at a time when state support for museums has been decreasing regularly. 'The Centre Pompidou's acquisition budget was €2 million [about £1.7 million] in 2018,' laments the French academic and art market specialist Alain Quemin. 'What can you buy with €2 million?'[5] he asks. (That figure was increased to €2.2 million in 2020.)[6]

The only way publicly funded museums can deal with this divergence in resources is to hope their board members and patrons will support acquisitions or, eventually, donate their art to the institution. This can also lead, however, to conflicts of interest, when patrons might exercise pressure on the museum to show their holdings or acquire artists in which they are themselves heavily 'invested'.

As well as the problem of rising prices, public museums may also be unable to hold the most prestigious exhibitions, simply because they cannot afford to stage them. Look at Paris's Fondation Louis Vuitton, which in 2021 was planning to bring 200 works from the fabulous Morozov collection to Paris from Russia, on loan from the State Hermitage Museum, St Petersburg, the Pushkin Museum of Fine Arts, Moscow and the State Tretyakov Gallery, Moscow.[7] That exhibition followed on from another blockbuster show, when in 2016–17 the same private, corporate-funded museum brought works from the Sergei Shchukin collection from the same Russian museums to Paris, attracting over 1.2 million visitors.[8] How many public institutions could stage such extraordinary shows – particularly in the post-pandemic period when their finances have collapsed?

Quemin comments:

> There is a competitive effect. In France, these very blockbuster shows were rather the monopoly of the Grand Palais and the

> Réunion des Musées Nationaux [French cultural umbrella organisation], but now Louis Vuitton for example has much deeper resources. And Bernard Arnault [owner of Louis Vuitton Moët Hennessy, which funds the museum] can offer exchanges from his own art collection, something that is far more difficult for the RMN.

He adds: 'A blockbuster show like the 2018–19 Jean-Michel Basquiat/ Egon Schiele shows at Vuitton[9] attracts the public, but at the same time private museums do rather undermine state institutions, because it means they can no longer do a Basquiat show.'

The opening of the Louis Vuitton Foundation is the best example in France of a private museum that directly competes with the country's most established public institutions which, until recently, had a quasi-monopoly over the most successful exhibitions. And as the museum-going public is not infinite, a sensational exhibition at a private art space can drain away visitors from the established institutions. 'Since the Vuitton Foundation opened, the Grand Palais has never had more than 500,000 visitors a year,' laments a leading Parisian museum director: 'If you add another exhibition venue, attendance will inevitably fall at other museums.'[10]

There is a greater tension as well in that private museums are often perceived, rightly or wrongly, as reflecting the gross inequalities in society today. 'Instead of being seen as a manifestation of the positive and progressive energies of civil society, private museums risk becoming emblems of inequity and billionaires run amok,' says Szántó.

Is this judgement wholly, partially, or not at all true? Are private museums a beneficial addition to the cultural landscape, despite a few less-than-honourable cases? In the following pages I examine the various forms they take, who their founders are, how they are financed and issues about their sustainability and legacy. I look also at the situation in China, where reports of a private museum 'boom' are true, but difficult to evaluate objectively. And finally, I wonder whether some wealthy collectors, with their impressive new museums, are capturing the cultural agenda as a function of their own tastes and personal interests. Can they skew the notions of the importance and value of their favoured artists, as far as their art historical and aesthetic significance is concerned?

1

What is a Private Museum?

The private collector's museum has become a highly visible and aspirational model for a growing number of influential wealthy collectors over the last two decades.

Georgina S. Walker, *The Private Collector's Museum: Public Good versus Private Gain*[1]

Today, the term 'private museum' covers a diverse range of institutions, from sculpture gardens or single-room displays to vast, architect-designed buildings funded by a luxury goods company or a real estate magnate. They tend to be primarily intended to house and display the founder's art collection, and generally lack the 'full services' of a publicly funded institution with conservation, research, education and curatorial departments.

In this book, the term 'private museum' is used to designate a not-for-profit art space, open to the public and established and funded primarily by an art collector and destined to show their collection. It may also designate a museum funded by a company, such as the three Pinault museums, two in Venice and one in Paris. In many cases private museums are used to display thematic exhibitions, with borrowed works shown alongside the core holdings. Some – following the Kunsthalle model – do not have the collection on show and hold exhibitions of loaned works, but often mixed with works from the founder's collection.

There is also a growing trend for artists to have their own museums – among them Damien Hirst, Bernar Venet, Thomas Schütte or Pierre Soulages. And finally, there are even a few museum 'chains', notably in China. The UCCA Center for Contemporary Art, for example, has three locations – Beijing, Shanghai and Beidaihe. The OCT Contemporary Art Terminal (OCAT) group is in four Chinese cities: Shanghai, Beijing, Xian and Shenzhen. François Pinault, as noted above, has three museums, two in Venice and one in Paris.

In fact, the very word 'museum' is problematic: this is a slippery term that means different things in different countries. In the United States, a museum is defined by the Office of the Federal Register as a public or private non-profit institution, open to the public, which owns and displays the objects in its care. These can be artworks, or anything else: for instance, ethnographic artefacts, wooden boats or even cable cars.

An additional problem is that virtually all American museums are 'private', in that they are not established and funded by the state, although they have charitable and tax-free status, and often some public funding. They must also conform to the guidelines laid down by professional bodies such as the American Alliance of Museums. 'Museums in this country are for the most part privately governed which isn't the same as privately owned,' says American art historian, curator and former museum director Maxwell Anderson: 'The Metropolitan Museum of Art is a public institution in that the building is owned by the city of New York, but the collection is owned by a private group of trustees. It is a bit of a hybrid situation, but we make the clear distinction in the USA that a private museum is typically classified as a foundation with 501(c)(3) status.'[2] We will come back to this in Chapter 3.

Private museums have existed since the 19th and early 20th centuries, and many early private museums survive to this day – London's Sir John Soane's Museum or Boston's Isabella Stewart Gardner Museum are just two examples. However, a characteristic of more recent creations is their emphasis on modern and contemporary art. Indeed, the International Committee for Museums and Collections of Modern Art

(CIMAM), part of the International Council of Museums (ICOM), which represents 20,000 museums from 136 countries, now admits private museums under certain conditions. They must be not-for-profit, have been open for over five years, comply with ICOM's code of ethics and have an appropriate governance structure.[3] Even so, fewer than 20 private museums are members, including UCCA in China and the Garage in Russia. This is not necessarily because others do not qualify, but because they may not have applied.

A key issue is governance. In many cases private museums have members of the family plus a couple of friends filling the board, with the owner-founder responsible for curating and acquisitions. While this is not necessarily a bad thing – and no-one can criticise a founder for deciding how the museum they pay for is run – sometimes interests can become blurred. 'The issues in contemporary art are complex because of the relationship with the market, the lack of regulation around the market and the potential way collectors can influence and sell works to their benefit,' explains Elizabeth Ann Macgregor, director of the Sydney Museum of Contemporary Art at the time of writing.[4]

In this book, I use 'private museum' as a catch-all term, although many founders eschew the term 'museum' itself: they call them foundations, institutes, collections, art spaces or centres, they may bear the name of a place or of the founder . . . anything but 'museum' in fact. Others, particularly in Asia, use the description widely. 'These are not "museums",' comments Anderson, stressing the 'not'. 'They are collections. The word "museum" is hallowed but is basically being bandied about now with ice cream museums and so on. As a result, it has lost a bit of meaning. The use of the word is in itself the value many founders are looking for – the anointment that accrues from having a "museum".'

Whatever the designation, I have limited this book to private museums which have a physical space, are accessible to the public and are not-for-profit, belong to a collector/founder or a corporation and have a collection of modern and contemporary art, either on view or from which items are drawn for exhibition. For the sake of simplicity, I use the term 'private museum' for all the forms they take.

So just how many private museums are there in the world? It is difficult to say exactly, since the number in China tends to evolve rapidly, but the 2018 edition of the *BMW Guide to Independent Collectors* lists 270 in 196 cities; of these, only four are in mainland China – obviously far short of the truth. Another listing, *The Private Art Museum Report* (PAMR), compiled by the website Larry's List with the aid of the Chinese company Art Market Monitor of Artron, covered 317 establishments in 2016, but of these just 26 were in China, which again is way short of the truth, even if the exact number is a shifting target. This report excludes corporate museums and only includes those belonging to living collectors. I think there are probably at least 400 across the world, although some do not have regular access but are open by appointment only.

What is astonishing is that of the 317 cited in the PAMR report, a stunning 70 per cent were founded after the year 2000; even more startingly, nearly one-fifth of these private spaces were built during the last five years. Just two museums in the listing were established before 1960. We shall return to the reasons why later in this book.

Why are almost all focused on contemporary art?

The reason is simple: today it is extremely difficult to create a museum of art in any historical field because there is just not enough supply of museum-quality material. There are a few exceptions, fuelled by determination and deep resources, such as The Leiden Collection of Dutch Old Masters, built up over 18 years by US financier Thomas Kaplan and his wife Daphne and which includes 17 Rembrandts (the collection is available online only, although it has been exhibited in various prestigious locations such as the Louvre in Paris and the Long private museum in Shanghai).[5] Another example is J. Tomilson Hill's hoard of Renaissance and Baroque bronzes. These are part of the hedge-fund mogul's holdings, which also comprise Old Master paintings and contemporary art, and which are displayed on rotation in his museum in New York's Chelsea district.[6]

Showing a personal collection to the public is not a new phenomenon; many of the world's best-loved museums evolved from private accumulations, for example the Frick Collection in New York (established in 1935). 'House' museums such as the Frick and others – for instance London's Wallace Collection (1897), which profoundly influenced Henry Frick[7]– were finally bequeathed to their respective nations and opened as public institutions. But today, wealthy collectors are increasingly retaining control of their art holdings by creating their own spaces. The reasons for this are varied and are examined in detail in Chapter 2.

* * *

Some museums are very small. An example is the Elliott Eyes collection, housed in the home of Gordon Elliott and Michael Eyes in Sydney, Australia. It was founded some 20 years ago in a Victorian townhouse, in which they live with their 300-object-strong collection, which almost overflows the space – even the bathrooms feature works of art. It is very eclectic, ranging from quirky ceramic animals to video, painting and neon, but with an emphasis on figurative art, although not exclusively so. The collectors have modest resources: Michael Eyes works in a bookshop and Gordon Elliott teaches line dancing. "Sometimes we have to pay off a purchase in instalments, when we can't afford something," says Elliott; he and his partner aim to meet every artist whose work they collect.[8] The collection is open to the public, who must pre-book, and Elliott or Eyes take visitors around themselves explaining many of the works and why they acquired them.

There are many other such small, collection-based spaces around the world, including the ultra-focused Le Silo, a collection of Minimalist art north of Paris, housed in a former grain silo. In Vancouver, Canada, the rennie museum shows the collection of real-estate mogul Bob Rennie in a historic building in Chinatown; in Barcelona, Spain, the Fundació Suñol displays, in a couple of rooms, the extensive collection of its founder Josep Suñol, from Balla or Giacometti to Picasso and

Miró. However, Suñol's death in 2019 was quickly followed by the sale of some significant pieces and the future of the museum was unclear at the time of writing (see Chapter 6).

At the other end of the spectrum are mega-projects such as The Broad in Los Angeles, established by local philanthropist and real estate developer Eli Broad, who died in 2021, and his wife Edythe. It displays their holdings of over 1500 works, now belonging to the foundation which runs the museum. It is housed in an iconic building designed by Diller Scofidio + Renfro, with a white mesh-like 'veil' covering the entire structure. Entry is free and the building also hosts temporary exhibitions.

In Miami, the Rubell Museum was inaugurated in late 2019, in a new 'campus' adapted from a series of warehouses and offering an expansive 100,000 square feet of space. Its inaugural exhibition consisted of 300 works by 100 artists – drawn from collectors Don and Mera Rubell's vast holdings of 7200 works by more than 1000 artists, probably the largest privately held assemblage of contemporary art in the United States. Even more commanding is GES-2 in Moscow, a converted power station near the Kremlin and the brainchild of billionaire Leonid Mikhelson. In scale, it surpasses London's Tate Modern. Originally destined to have a grand opening in 2020, its inauguration was delayed by the COVID-19 crisis to late 2021.

Private museums tend to be of two extremes – small and personal on the one hand and immense on the other – but between are a plethora of spaces, some in repurposed buildings, others in custom-built structures. Their founders may take a close – sometimes too close – interest in the curation, or leave the buying and administration up to advisors. Some may have independent governance, others just family members.

Company museums – a branding exercise

Among the most spectacular of today's new private museums are those built by fashion and luxury goods groups, notably Bernard Arnault's Louis Vuitton Moët Hennessy (LVMH) and Kering, belonging to

François Pinault. This industry is dominated by just these two vastly rich groups, who own a plethora of brands – and have given the world a number of private museums, including the Fondazione Prada in Milan, as well as the Fondation Louis Vuitton in Paris.

The founders of these corporate museums are generally collectors themselves, the prime example being that of Pinault, who rose from a modest background in rural France to become one of the world's richest men (worth $46 billion in 2021, according to Forbes).[9] His sprawling empire includes Kering (wine, watches and fashion houses Gucci, Saint Laurent etc.), Christie's auction house and other investments. He also has about 10,000 works of contemporary art and in the early 2000s attempted to establish a museum in Paris, on an abandoned site on an island in the Seine river. Frustrated by local opposition and administrative delays, he pulled out of this project and bought the 17th-century Palazzo Grassi in Venice for €29 million.[10] Then two years later, in 2007, Pinault acquired Punta della Dogana, a former customs warehouse on the tip of the island of Dorsoduro, on the Grand Canal just opposite the Piazza San Marco. This was rented for 33 years from the Venetian authorities. A third museum in Paris, the Bourse du Commerce, opened in 2021.

'A company-backed private museum has to be successful because otherwise it has an impact on the brand,' comments cultural consultant Sébastien Montabonel:

> They have to make it good because it is a brand exercise – it is linked to their business. The challenge of companies like Prada is to be perceived as a luxury brand rather than a mass market one. By affiliating themselves with the art world, it helps them to project an image that is now truly top end; in addition, the only time Prada gets press coverage is during catwalks, but everyone is getting attention then. With a big, smart museum you keep the name in front of the public and get attention 365 days a year.[11]

Certainly, the biggest and smartest of these company museums is the Fondation Louis Vuitton's building in Paris. This was rebuilt by Frank Gehry for LVMH on an existing, outdated and abandoned museum, to the tune of €780 million in 2017.[12] It is clearly also a machine for promoting the brand, with the shiny LV logo affixed on the entrance and a group of antique leather Vuitton trunks protruding from a wall. Bernard Arnault, the owner of the parent company LVMH, was the third richest person in the world in 2021, with $150 billion, according to Forbes. Much has been made of the rivalry between Pinault and Arnault, who fell out in 2001 with the battle for Gucci (Pinault won[13]), and now their museums look like proxy weapons: why should Pinault need a third museum, except to challenge Arnault on his home turf?

From office blocks to shopping malls

In 2019 I made the long journey from the UK to Jakarta to visit a private museum established by the Indonesian businessman Haryanto Adikoesoemo, one of the richest men in the country. His space, MACAN (pronounced 'Machan') is Indonesia's first museum of modern and contemporary art but is housed in two floors of an office block owned by Adikoesoemo, a way, he said, of saving on rent. On the ground floor are restaurants and a FamilyMart. The museum shows a selection of his 800-strong collection, plus a temporary exhibition (when I visited, there was a retrospective of the renowned Chinese artist Xu Bing[14]). Adikoesoemo's holdings range from the best-known Indonesian artists such as Nyoman Masriadi to international favourites such as Damien Hirst or Gerhard Richter. He told me one of his reasons for opening a museum: 'Even five years ago there were little alternatives for entertainment for a family here, outside going to the mall.'[15]

There was a just a smattering of visitors when I was there, but Adikoesoemo has hired a good curator – former museum director Aaron Seeto – to sort through his eclectic holdings and put the museum on a more conventional footing. Adikoesoemo himself was charming and open but his comments seemed more focused on the tax and investment aspects of his collection. Time will tell as to what extent MACAN will make an impact on the cultural landscape in Indonesia.

While the idea of a museum in a mall may raise eyebrows in some places, it is a growing trend around the world: in Beirut, New Delhi, Shanghai or even Poznan in Poland, retail owners have seized on culture as a way of attracting shoppers and retaining them longer, increasing what the trade calls 'dwell time'. Probably the most prominent is the K11 Art Mall in Hong Kong, created by the art collector and retail billionaire Adrian Cheng. K11 currently has exhibition and event spaces called 'Chi Art Spaces' in Shanghai, Guangzhou, Shenyang and Hong Kong 'to showcase art and cultural exhibitions and special events', according to a spokesperson; the cultural-retail concept, as it is called, is due to be extended to 35 projects.[16] The Shanghai venue sits in the third basement of a glitzy mall boasting luxury goods stores and, in the past, has hosted exhibitions of Katharina Grosse and Zhang Enli; it has also collaborated with London's Serpentine Gallery and Paris's Palais de Tokyo.

Similar thinking – using a museum to attract shoppers – was behind the Lebanese collector and retail magnate Tony Salamé's project, Aïshti, in Beirut. The 'art-cum-shopping mall' was inaugurated in September 2015, in an eye-catchingly blingy building, all angular black-and-white designs and mirrors, designed by David Adjaye. The museum, attached to the mall, even has glass windows onto the shops; it shows highlights of Salamé's 2500-strong collection. Despite the devastating explosion in Beirut's port in 2020, when the museum just suffered some broken windows, and the 2020–21 Covid crisis, the museum was open at the time of writing in 2021.[17]

Does all this mean that museums in malls and office buildings should be dismissed as mere bait for shoppers? Not at all – for a start, in countries with few private museums, they fulfil an educational role the state cannot assume. In India, the Kiran Nadar Museum of Art in South Court Mall, Saket, New Delhi, offers visitors the chance to see contemporary Indian and Pakistani art as well as traditional Indian miniatures and modernist paintings. Jakarta's MACAN has been able to give a platform to Indonesian artists. And, while their quality varies greatly, Chinese museums in malls can bring a new generation to culture, a generation with no tradition of museum going. As Adrian Cheng told me in 2016: 'Walking into a "white cube" is not only intimidating, it is a foreign experience based on a concept that has not been ingrained in the psyches of most Chinese. So we bring the art to them in a setting they already know.'[18]

Sculpture parks

Finally, there has been a growing fashion for art collectors to establish sculpture or art parks. Certainly, the most spectacular and magical is Inhotim in Brumadinho, Brazil, a true 'destination' but not easily accessible; it is almost two hours by road from Belo Horizonte airport, which itself is hardly on most tourists' itineraries. Nevertheless, the park attracted three million visitors in 2018.

Here, local mining millionaire-collector Bernardo Paz commissioned multiple well-known artists to make site-specific works for a 5000-acre, highly praised botanical garden. The gardens were designed by Brazilian landscape architect Roberto Burle Marx; dotted around them are pavilions housing works of art and site-specific open-air sculptures by over 500 noted Brazilian and international artists. These include Hélio Oiticica, Adriana Varejão (also one of Paz's five ex-wives), Chris Burden, Yayoi Kusama, Anish Kapoor, Thomas Hirschhorn, Doug Aitken, Dominique Gonzalez-Foerster, Steve McQueen, Cildo Meireles and Vik Muniz.

When I met him in 2013, Paz lived up to his reputation as an eccentric, failing to answer questions or giving irrelevant answers in a whisper, obviously bored by meeting journalists. With his shoulder-length grey hair, white beard and flowing linen clothing, he looked a bit hippy-like. However, his park more than compensated for his apparent indifference, with the ambitious artworks carefully placed in and around the lush vegetation and extensive views across the perfectly manicured landscaping to the surrounding hills.

In 2017 Paz was found guilty and sentenced to nine years in prison for money-laundering, for allegedly using almost $100 million, supposedly destined to support Inhotim, to pay expenses and debts for his businesses. On appeal, he was acquitted of all charges in 2020.[19] With his reputation cleared, Paz might have continued his plans to expand the park and build ten hotels around the site, but the Covid pandemic struck, hitting Brazil particularly badly. In early 2021 Inhotim was closed to the public, but reopened to visitors in the early summer.

There are hundreds of sculpture parks in the world, both private and public, and most museums include an outdoor display area for their acquisitions. Among those specifically created as art parks this century is Château La Coste, near Aix-en-Provence in the south of France, established by the Irish property magnate Paddy McKillen. This features commissioned works by Tadao Ando, Liam Gillick, Sean Scully, Hiroshi Sugimoto and Louise Bourgeois, and is linked to a winery and very expensive luxury hotel.

In Scotland, Nicky and Robert Wilson surrounded their 17th-century manor outside Edinburgh with site-specific artworks, the best-known being Charles Jencks's sculpted mounds of grass, *Cells of Life* (2008–10), which encircle four small lakes: they are the first thing visitors see when they arrive. The park, Jupiter Artland, is open to the public in the summer and to school groups in the winter; visitors pay to enter, but Jupiter is a registered charity, subsidised by ticket sales and donations.

Near Oslo, collector Christen Sveaas converted a family paper mill into a sculpture garden and museum called Kistefos, after his investment company. By the mill, an octopus-like red and white spotted work by Yayoi Kusama bobs in the water while, further down, the fast-flowing river gushes through a circular Marc Quinn sculpture, made in the form of the iris of Sveaas's eye. Sveaas linked the two riverbanks with The Twist, an 'inhabitable bridge' designed by the Danish architect Bjarke Ingels that actually twists as it crosses the water; it is used as an exhibition space, for Sveaas's own collection and for borrowed works.

In many cases, these art parks also stimulate the local economy. This was certainly one, if not the main, reason why the Wilsons established Jupiter Artland outside Edinburgh. And The Twist should bring visitors to the little town of Jevnaker, 80 km from Oslo. But for the most spectacular success in urban renewal and an example of how such parks can transform the local economy, one must go to a private museum in Tasmania, Australia: I will talk about it in the next chapter.

2

The Founders and their Motivations

Who is the great collector? Is it that wealthy, established aristocrat with the great deal of land, a great deal of money, or is it the self-made?

Sir Mark Jones, former director of the Victoria and Albert Museum, London[1]

When you have individuals of great means, there will always be multiple ambitions and aspirations.

András Szántó, cultural consultant[2]

According to the *Private Art Museum Report*, the overwhelming majority of museum founders today are male (81 per cent), with an average age of 65.[3] However, this finding only tells part of the story, since it is quantitative rather than qualitative and some of the most admired private museums today were started by female collectors. The report dates from 2016, and an updated version was in preparation at the time of writing.

Examples of these female collectors include Patrizia Sandretto Re Rebaudengo (Fondazione Sandretto Re Rebaudengo in Turin, Italy); Maja Hoffman with the LUMA Foundation in Arles, France; Grażyna Kulczyk who established the Muzeum Susch in the lower Engadin valley in the Swiss Alps; Julia Stoschek (with her collection of video art, shown in Düsseldorf and Berlin, Germany); Judith Neilson (White Rabbit Gallery in Sydney, Australia); Anita Zabludowicz, whose project space is housed in a former Methodist chapel in London; or Miuccia Prada, co-chair of the company-funded Fondazione Prada in Milan, Italy and a collector in her own right.

Then many private museums have been founded by couples. Indeed, the common interest and goals they share create a powerful bond – and there is even good reason to believe that art can provide the 'glue' in a marriage. The Miami-based collector Mera Rubell put it bluntly in 2015, when she stated: 'The fact of the matter is that it [art] saved our marriage, it brought us together, it saved our family, because it's constantly teaching us about who we are, and somehow giving hope that there's a future.'[4]

The wealth factor

The one thing these collectors have in common, obviously, is wealth: enough money to build an art collection and then put it on display, whether in their own home, in a repurposed building or a specially designed one. 'The rise of the private museum is certainly about people having more and more money: the rich have become richer and richer, and so the available surplus has grown and grown.' So says Sir Mark Jones; he continues:

> We are talking hundreds of millions and sometimes billions of dollars expended on art. It seems to be a clear case of competitive consumption. Like all creatures, human beings are driven by a desire to emphasise their fitness in evolutionary terms. And, according to handicap theory exemplified by the peacock's tail, they do this by showing that they are strong enough and powerful enough to expend resources on explicitly useless activities.

Jones references the American sociologist Thorstein Veblen's *The Theory of the Leisure Classes*, an 1899 critique of society, notably its emphasis on conspicuous consumption as a means of distinguishing oneself with ostentatious display. Veblen's book was written at the end of America's Gilded Age and was both an economic and social critique of that age. This three-decades-long period of huge economic growth in the late 19th century saw a high concentration of wealth but also vast inequality. It witnessed the rise of populism and corruption, both in politics and in business, but also of 'new philanthropy' with the birth of the private foundation, administered by private, self-governing trustees with paid professional staffs.

Andrew Carnegie and John D. Rockefeller were among those who established foundations and endowed libraries, universities and museums – 'out of a mix of altruism and the self-preservational desire to cool public anger [at wealth inequality],' snipes Anand Giridharadas in his 2019 book *Winners Take All*.[5] Whatever their motivations, their legacy has been preserved in some of the best-endowed and most celebrated art museums in the world: New York's Metropolitan Museum of Art and the Frick Collection, among others. And the unscrupulous methods some of the Gilded Age philanthropists had originally used to get rich are now often forgotten.

In some ways we are living in a new Gilded Age today, with huge fortunes but increasing inequality and, again, the rise of populism as the 'left-behind' manifest their anger and resentment. Examples are the short-lived Occupy Wall Street movement and, more long-term, the election of populist politicians around the world. Just as the names of the great philanthropists of the past live on through their charitable works, no doubt some of the most notable private museum founders of today – such as Eli Broad – will gain similar permanency. Sir Mark again: 'The private museum is likely to go on carrying your name and conserving your collections and providing prestige for longer than the alternative, such as a gift to a big institution which has its own agenda, which won't necessarily coincide with yours.'

Commenting on the rise of private museums, the cultural consultant Adrian Ellis notes:

These extremely wealthy people have lots of money to play with, but they don't know what to do with it! One of the ways in which they solve this annoying problem is to buy art – it's a form of conspicuous consumption which also brings a rise in social standing, it's fun and bizarrely it has become a relatively secure form of wealth. The physicality of art has become one of its assets – you can put in your warehouse or museum.[6]

That wealth of museum founders may be inherited, in which case there is often, but not always, a tradition of art collecting in the family. An example of this is Maja Hoffmann, an heiress of the Swiss pharmaceutical giant Fritz Hoffmann-La Roche.

His granddaughter, Maja Hoffmann – rather shy, determined, dark-haired and half-Russian – established the LUMA Foundation in Arles in 2004. It is sited on a 15-acre former railway yard, an area that had become an abandoned eyesore until Hoffmann – who grew up in nearby Camargue – took it over. At one end is the extraordinary, Frank Gehry-designed tower. The 56-metre-tall glittering edifice – sometimes unkindly compared to a crumpled soft drink can – consists of a series of stainless-steel slabs arranged to look like a jagged cliff. Under its gleaming facade, the site comprises six industrial sheds – refurbished by the experienced art gallery and museum designer Annabelle Selldorf – which house temporary exhibitions as well as the annual photography event Les Rencontres d'Arles. The overall cost to Hoffmann is over $175 million, all funded by her.[7] The whole project houses exhibitions, workshops, residencies and artists' studios as well as a 10-acre public park. That is not all; locally, Hoffmann is president of the Arles Van Gogh museum, has created two boutique hotels and owns a Michelin-starred restaurant, La Chassagnette. She also sits on the boards of over a dozen museums and art institutions worldwide, including London's Serpentine Galleries, New York's New Museum and the Center for Curatorial Studies at Bard College in New York State.

Despite the obvious cultural, social and economic benefits for the town, the LUMA project has been controversial. Hoffmann is creating more than a private museum, rather an 'ideal city' with hotels, restaurants and public spaces, and has preserved, renovated and renewed many of the historical structures in the vicinity. But, in realising all of this, and with enormous resources, Hoffmann has battled town planners, a conflicted Communist mayor and opposition from the former director of the Rencontres d'Arles, François Hébel, who resigned in protest at what he saw as excessive powers on her part.[8] And the *Financial Times* singled out for harsh criticism LUMA's centrepiece, Le Parc des Ateliers, as one of a series of 'franchised modern art museums', calling them 'expensively and immaculately bland'. 'It makes the sensation of visiting modern art museums uncomfortably like the luxury industry,' the piece continued, 'with which art is closely aligned. Similar Louis Vuitton and Gucci flagship stores are planted across prime shopping districts in Hong Kong, Los Angeles or Dubai, groomed and gleaming. Renovated warehouses and power stations have become the art world's equivalent.'[9] The article – and the unflattering image accompanying it – apparently stung Hoffmann deeply.[10]

In contrast, many of the founders of private museums are new billionaires: Forbes listed 2755 billionaires in the world in 2021, some of them holding staggering fortunes.[11] In early 2021 Elon Musk became the world's richest man with $185 billion, although rankings at the top change rapidly, with Jeff Bezos close behind.[12] Bernard Arnault was worth over $150 billion in 2021 and Alice Walton $66 billion, again according to Forbes. Both have art collections and have built museums: Alice Walton has spent vast sums on her Crystal Bridges Museum of American Art in the out-of-the-way town of Bentonville, Arkansas. Or there is the Mexican telecoms billionaire Carlos Slim (worth $62.8 billion in 2021, according to Forbes) who shows his profuse but eclectic and patchy art holdings at the ramshackle Museo Soumaya in Mexico City, a building that stands in stark contrast to the elegant, carefully curated Museo Jumex just across the road – also a private museum, founded by Eugenio López, heir to a foodstuffs fortune.

Today the billionaire's ultimate trophy is a massively expensive work of art, easily beating yachts, mega-mansions and Ferraris. Just look at the stupendous price paid in 2018 for Leonardo da Vinci's *Salvador Mundi* (*c.*1500) – $450.3 million, a sum paid not by an established art collector but reportedly by the Crown Prince of Saudi Arabia, Sheikh Mohammed bin Salman (often known by his initials MBS). Its ultimate destination, true owner and indeed location were not clear at the time of writing, although a 2021 film, *The Savior for Sale,* affirmed it belongs to the Saudi Arabian Ministry of Culture.[13] Why it has not gone on show, despite being promised initially for the 2019–20 Leonardo da Vinci exhibition at the Louvre,[14] has not been entirely explained either. While nothing near that level been sold at the time of writing, Sandro Botticelli's *Portrait of a Young Man Holding a Roundel* of *c.*1480 made $92.1 million in 2021, reportedly going to a Russian buyer, having been consigned for sale by American collector Sheldon Solow, who died in 2020 (see Chapter 3).[15]

The 'outsider' status

According to Sir Mark Jones, collecting has always been a way for self-made people to affirm their success. 'This is one of the ways in which people who are outsiders can, to an extent, challenge or overcome their outsider status,' he told me. 'If you look at a collection, like [London's] Wallace collection – Richard Wallace was an outsider, because of being illegitimate, because of being married to a perfumer's assistant.' He continued:

> If you think about the preponderance of Jewish collectors in Russia or in the United States or, indeed, in Britain – they are outside the mainstream. If you think about 'Who is the great collector?', is it that wealthy, established aristocrat with the great deal of land, a great deal of money, or is it the self-made?

An example of such a self-made fortune can be found in post-Communist Russia. Leonid Mikhelson is among the country's richest men and he has created GES-2 – part exhibition space, part cultural venue – in Moscow, close to the Kremlin, in a former power station which has been extensively refurbished by the Italian architect Renzo Piano. At the time of writing, its opening was delayed by the Covid pandemic and no new date fixed. Mikhelson, who is reported to be close to the Russian president Vladimir Putin, made his vast fortune in natural gas; after the fall of the Soviet Union, he bought a stake in a privatised pipeline construction company, which eventually became publicly listed.[16] Comparisons with London's Tate Modern, another converted power station, seem inevitable though GES-2 is even bigger, boasting 40,000 square metres of internal space, beating Tate's 34,500 square metres.

'My parents had no interest in art,' Mikhelson told me. 'But even before I established the [V-A-C] foundation and the museum, I was collecting – I started with classic 18th-century paintings, then Impressionists – and then I started getting interested in contemporary art.'[17] His collection, on permanent loan to the Moscow-based V-A-C Foundation, comprises about 300 modern and contemporary works by artists such as Amedeo Modigliani, Francis Bacon, Sigmar Polke, Christopher Wool, Wade Guyton and Lucy McKenzie, along with major 20th-century Russian artists such as Natalia Goncharova or Wassily Kandinsky.

Over the past few years, I have interviewed the founders of private museums, seeking to find out how they started collecting, how their collection evolved, and why and how they moved from having their own holdings to putting them on public display. No two cases are the same, but I found that a clear majority of the private museum owners I spoke to come from families with no interest in art, or at least no art in their homes, like Mikhelson. This is partly because many come from countries where art collecting was unheard of in the 20th century for political reasons, or because their fortune is self-made and their family background lacked the sort of wealth that would have enabled them to buy art. Indeed, some parents were shocked when their son or daughter started spending serious sums on what they considered a wasteful hobby.

Across the world, I heard the same story: in Indonesia Haryanto Adikoesoemo said that, in his case, his father was horrified by his collecting, thinking that he would be 'conned by the galleries'. 'He just didn't understand how you could pay so much money for a work of art!' he said.[18] Even François Pinault, one of the world's major collectors, as well as being among the world's wealthiest men through his luxury goods company Kering, comes from a simple family in the timber business in Brittany, certainly not one with any interest in the arts.

So what are the reasons that push collectors like these to spend so heavily on their own private museums? According to London-based wealth manager Steven Kettle, partner at Stonehage Fleming, who advises clients on succession planning for art collections – including when they are thinking of founding a private museum – 'Their number one consideration is to keep the collection together.' And, he adds, 'They also don't like giving up control.'[19]

Control and trust

This question of control is significant. Today's art collectors, those who have established their own museums, have often, if not always, made their money themselves, often in finance, real estate, retail or manufacturing. They are accustomed to making their own decisions, they have created the collection and they want to manage its display, curation and lending. Relinquishing power goes against their fundamental instincts.

'Giving to a public institution represents loss of control and I suspect that is the thing that makes collectors stay their hand more than anything else,' says Adrian Ellis:

> Most public institutions are reluctant to meet the sort of conditions that private givers want. When museum directors talk to potential donors, the latter will ask questions such as, 'Will it be deaccessioned, will it have its own separate space, and will it have my name on it?' Public institutions are reluctant to meet these conditions because of their own internal policies – so pretty soon the collector thinks, 'Why don't I have some fun now and make my own museum?'

The Dutch collector Han Nefkens, who does not have his own museum but who places video works, photography, painting, sculpture and installations with institutions as long-term loans and promised gifts, told me: 'The reason I don't give immediately is because, and I would like a nicer word, of control. To be sure it is being shown regularly and in the proper conditions.' And he requires that works he has loaned be shown every five years.[20]

An astonishing admission comes from Sir Mark, who told me: 'Well, you'd be pretty mad to give it to the British Museum or the Victoria and Albert. Because what will happen is that it will disappear over time. Some of these museums are in the habit of breaking people's wills. They know they can do this and, in the end, they do.' And he adds: 'The idea that you're going to have a gallery permanently in your name, it's an illusion. You might have it for a bit, but after a while it too will disappear.' There is also the question of trust. Collectors fear that public institutions might not treat the collection as they would, nor conserve it correctly and keep it on display. In the United States, there is the added concern, among donors, that a work of art could be deaccessioned.

Such are these fears that Doris and Don Fisher, founders of The Gap clothing brand, kept a firm rein on the loan of their billion-dollar collection of contemporary art to San Francisco Museum of Modern Art (SFMOMA) in 2010. They had initially tried, but failed, to create their own museum in the Presidio district, but this was rejected for environmental reasons.[21] Having decided to lend to SFMOMA, they underwrote the construction of a new wing of the museum, while at the same time putting extraordinarily stringent conditions on the loan of over 1000 works. They stipulated that the loan would be for 100 years, renewable for another 25, after which their descendants would decide on the fate of the collection. The works would have to be shown with a 75 per cent to 25 per cent ratio of Fisher to non-Fisher works, and every ten years the museum had to mount a show exclusively of the Fisher collection. 'These conditions mean the collection is frozen and already looking old fashioned – and losing relevance; and it is generally not well attended,' says a prominent British museum director, requesting anonymity.[22]

Even if the agreement between institution and donor is laid down in a careful contract, donors fear that the terms could be broken at some point in the future. A glaring example is that of the Barnes Foundation in Philadelphia, where the admittedly quirky terms of the founder's will were finally overturned after decades of wrangling. The financially strapped institution, holding legendary riches that included 170 Renoirs, 55 Cézannes and 20 Picassos, was moved from its Philadelphia suburb to a more central location in the city in 2011, after a judge broke the trust established by Albert C. Barnes.[23] More recently, London's Wallace Collection was able to loan works out for the first time, after lawyers and art experts 're-examined' the terms of Lady Wallace's will.[24]

Two things are exacerbating this breakdown of trust. One is the – perfectly laudable – desire of museums to reflect diversity. In order to buy works by women and artists of colour, in 2019 SFMOMA sold a Mark Rothko painting for $50.1 million, using the proceeds to buy works by 11 artists. The decision was controversial, as the Rothko had been donated by the artist himself; other museums in the US and elsewhere have also sold works, for similar reasons.[25]

Selling works can also be a way of generating much-needed revenue. When the 2020 pandemic hit museums across the world, they were forced to close for the large part of a year. Without takings from ticketing, events, shops and cafes, museums faced massive shortfalls – for example, Tate's self-generated income (for its two galleries in London and others in Liverpool and St Ives) was expected to be down by £56 million in the financial year ending April 2021. It had generated £94 million in 2019–20, so the harsh drop amounted to 60 per cent. A similar tale was told elsewhere: the Victoria and Albert Museum suffered a 63 per cent fall in self-generated income over the same period; worse, the British Museum saw its visitor-generated proceeds plummet by more than 90 per cent of the projected sum, a figure the museum was not prepared to divulge.[26]

In the United States, the American Association of Museum Directors revised its rules in 2020 so that museums could sell art, for the 'direct care' of their holdings.[27] The Brooklyn Museum became one of a number of institutions to take advantage of this relaxation of the rules and quickly sent 12 works to auction, including a 1921 bequest, Lucas Cranach the Elder's 16th-century *Lucretia*. It sold at Christie's New York in October 2020 for $5.1 million.[28] Such deaccessions – there were a number in 2020, including other works that were originally donated – raise fears amongst potential donors that their gifts could suffer the same fate.

Public value and 'giving back to the community'

There is a great deal of difference between collecting for oneself and one's home and deciding to put one's collection on view in a publicly accessible space. The decision will inevitably entail choices about the ultimate destination of family wealth, and the involvement (or not) of heirs, but also the extent to which collecting changes. A personal, quirky assemblage is one thing – but once a collector is buying for a 'museum' or a space open to the public, their focus often shifts, since they are now looking not only with their own eyes, but with the eyes of the outside world. They may find themselves looking to 'fill the gaps' rather than just buying what they like. In a 2019 interview, Dr Christoph Becker, Director of the Kunsthaus Zürich, said: 'As long as it [the art collection] remains in your private home or is in storage, it remains private, but if you go public things change. It is no longer you and the artworld – it is the public and the work of art . . . The public takes away what you have built and consumes it – it is no longer yours.'[29]

Mera Rubell told me:

> I would say when we first took the collection public it totally paralysed us. It froze us because we had a dilemma – we thought about all the art we didn't have and for a while it took the fun out of collecting. We couldn't be who we were. People could walk in and say: 'Where is your [Jasper] Johns?' – and we were showing Keith Haring. But one day we had a family session and we said, we have to celebrate who we are, and this is what we do.[30]

According to art historian and curator Maxwell Anderson: 'Motivations are always a mixture – it's the human comedy, people have variations of impulse and intent. The Rubells are art lovers who want to see their collection in the public realm, it's not that they don't get fun as well, but the overarching value to the public is far in excess of the value to them.'[31]

Variations on the theme of 'giving back to the community' was the reason most cited by the museum founders I met. Christen Sveaas explained why he had established The Twist outside Oslo in Norway (see Chapter 1): 'I believe if you have been successful, then you should help others to be successful, that is the greatest happiness,' he said. 'It was to justify that I've been lucky – and to give something back.'[32]

Then there is a genuine desire to give a platform to contemporary art and artists in countries where the government cannot fund contemporary art museums. In countries such as India, Indonesia or Bangladesh, private museums are essential to give contemporary artists visibility in the absence of government support and interest. In Italy, public institutions largely ignore contemporary art, leaving foundations such as the highly acclaimed Fondazione Sandretto Re Rebaudengo in Turin to fill this gap. And, in many cases, such museums also run educational programmes, making up for the lack of such provision in the state sector.

Rajeeb Samdani says his aim is to support Bengali artists and bring international artists to the country. He and his wife Nadia established the biennial Dhaka Art Summit in 2012, putting the city on the art-world map and giving local artists a platform that did not exist before. He told me:

> Before we established the Summit, there was no destination in South Asia where people could see art from around the world. Anyone can buy art and put it somewhere – saying, 'Come and see!' But that is not our main agenda – it is to build local awareness for contemporary art, to focus on education and have a location and space where local audiences and international audiences can come from all over the world.[33]

The Samdanis are also establishing an art space and museum, Srihatta, in Sylhet, Bangladesh, with a sculpture garden and a major focus on artist residencies: 'We want to invite artists, curators, museum directors, and we are already commissioning work, even though the space is not yet completed,' says Samdani.

In the case of Patrizia Sandretto Re Rebaudengo, her Fondazione in Turin stands as an exemplary model of patronage, educational ambitions and support for artists. She told me that when she started it in 1995:

> In Italy, apart from an important contemporary art museum such as Castello di Rivoli, there were still no institutions specifically dedicated to the new artistic generation. I realized that if I wanted to be more than just a collector, to be more involved, I didn't want to build a house of my collection, I wanted to give the opportunity to everybody to learn more about contemporary art. And particularly because at the time there was very little education in this field.[34]

Over the years since it was founded, the foundation has seen 25,000 children attend sessions at the six-person-strong education department. Now, Sandretto says, she is seeing adults who visited as children come back with their own offspring.

Another example is that of Anita Zabludowicz, who was born in the north of England. Along with her businessman husband Poju, from Finland, she decided to collect art in the mid-1990s. In 2007 they inaugurated an unusual exhibition space in a former 19th-century Methodist chapel in North London. It shows curated projects drawn from the collection, which spans international art since the 1960s, but is more focused on European and North American artists from the 1990s onwards. Zabludowicz also commissions exhibitions, working with artists at pivotal moments in their careers, and in 2018 founded the UK's first dedicated exhibition programme for virtual reality (VR) artworks.

Working closely with curator Elizabeth Neilson, who has been with her since 2006, Zabludowicz is known for discovering and supporting emerging artists, notably by funding production of contemporary works, often not even acquiring the finished piece. But Zabludowicz goes far beyond that, eschewing 'market darlings': 'So boring – all those swathes of paintings at art fairs!' she says. She is also extremely philanthropic, benefitting a wide range of public institutions: for example, sponsoring the education programme at Camden Arts Centre, assisting with Tate purchases, as well as sitting as a trustee on numerous boards. In addition, she has created an artist residency and art park on the tiny Finnish island of Sarvisalo. In 2015 she was awarded the British honour of OBE, for services to the arts.

Speaking before the 2020 pandemic closed such activities, Zabludowicz explained:

> Our aim is to be learning-focused: the majority of our outreach is working with artists to extend and support their art practice; we also work closely with the local community and have artist-led workshops with local families with young children coming in on weekends to do projects in relation to the exhibitions. There are also specially commissioned performances, talks, films and lectures around every exhibition we do, mainly aimed at artists and art professionals.[35]

However, the Zabludowiczs have been criticised for their pro-Israel stance, the source of their fortune – supplying arms to Israel – and their ties to the Israeli state. After the May 2021 conflict between Gaza and Israel there were renewed calls for a boycott of the Zabludowicz Art Trust and 25 artists announced they were 'deauthoring' works they had made for the collection.[36]

Zabludowicz and Sandretto Re Rebaudengo are far from the only collectors to focus on outreach to the community. One other example is the Rosa and Carlos de la Cruz Collection in Miami, which funds annual scholarships for students at the local high school and sends 40 students a year to the School of Visual Arts and Parsons School of Design in New York. Significantly, their website notes that: 'The collection is not a 501(c)(3) and does not receive government assistance.'[37] (See Chapter 3 for an explanation of 501(c)(3)s.)

Urban regeneration: the 'Bilbao effect'

Private art museums can also contribute to invigorating the local environment – known as the 'Bilbao effect', after the Guggenheim established a museum in 1997 in the Spanish city of Bilbao, revitalising the ailing port city.[38] This is the case in Florida, where the city of Miami has been transformed by local collectors such as the Rubells, Rosa and Carlos de la Cruz, real estate developer Craig Robins and Martin Margulies, another real estate developer whose collection, spanning Abstract Expressionism to contemporary art, is housed in a huge former warehouse in the Wynwood district. Since then, the previously 'no-go' wasteland of warehouses and drug dealers has been transformed into a chic, upmarket 'design district' boasting craft breweries, fashion boutiques and art galleries.

The 'Bilbao effect' can also be seen on the other side of the world in Hobart, the capital of the state of Tasmania, an island off the southern tip of Australia. But before 2011 it was neither sexy nor cool – rather the target of bus tours and caravans. Then that year David Walsh established the Museum of Old and New Art (MONA), built hotels and residences around it and regenerated the whole area. Visits to the island rose from just over 900,000 in 2010 to over 3.5 million in 2019, with 1.2 million of them flocking to Hobart alone.[39]

Walsh is an eccentric – a multi-millionaire and the leader of what Australian newspapers describe as the world's biggest gambling syndicate, Bank Roll. The museum is almost entirely built underground, with an emphasis on the erotic, the exotic and the puerile: it features a wall of sculptures of women's vulvas, racks of rotting cow carcasses and, most famously, Wim Delvoye's *Cloaca Professional* (2010), a machine that turns food into faeces, which it excretes daily. Walsh has said that guilt at his success largely motivated the desire to build the museum: 'Winning gamblers,' he wrote in his 2014 autobiography *A Bone of Fact*; 'end up with money but have achieved nothing else. It's fair to argue that I built Mona to absolve myself from feeling guilty about making money without making a mark.'[40]

The darker side

There may be other, more complicated, elements at play. Some might be understandable, particularly in the case of founders who have come from modest backgrounds and are now able to 'share' their good fortune with the public. They have succeeded, and the outwardly visible signs of their riches are their art collection and the other toys of success: a big house, cars, yachts and maybe even a football team. According to Sir Mark: 'I have never ever come across a collector who didn't want to show their stuff off – that's the whole point of having it, isn't it?'

This aspect cannot be underestimated, alongside an often healthy competitiveness. This is unsurprising, considering that many of the private museum owners I interviewed were self-made individuals, whose success was certainly the result of a finely honed instinct to win – and the belief that they knew best. The Belgian collector Walter Vanhaerents even saw other collectors as competitors and told me that 'there is a fight' to get the best pieces. One of his main motivations, in setting up his own art space, was gaining better access to the works of art he wanted.[41]

Indeed, this question of access – to the best pieces, the most in-demand artists – is an aspect of private museums rarely evoked by those I interviewed, but is most likely a significant motivation. For the most sought-after artists – and those whose prices are on an upward trajectory – a collector cannot just walk into a gallery or fair booth and buy a work of art. The dealer will often not even give a price in the first instance, before enquiring more about the potential buyer. This is to prevent 'flipping' – rapid resale at a profit, which the dealer cannot control – and also to establish whether the sale is in the interest of the artist. Will the work go into a 'good' collection or, better still, into a museum? Public display, or being chosen by a known collector, enhances the artist's profile – so owning one's own space is a telling argument for access.

This aspect has been exploited in the past when unscrupulous buyers have used the excuse of a 'museum' or 'foundation' to obtain heavy discounts or access to prized works. The Swiss dealer Pierre Huber was accused of this after he dumped 74 works of contemporary art into a Christie's sale in New York in 2007, making $16.8 million. Dealers and artists expressed outrage, saying Huber had led them to believe he was building a collection that would eventually end up in a museum, and had got huge discounts in return. At the time, Huber shrugged off the criticism, saying: 'The art market is a market like every market. You can't blackmail the collector, telling him, "You can buy but you can never sell."'[42]

Another charge often levelled at private museums is that they are merely vanity projects aimed at avoiding tax obligations, as well as showing off the collection – and, in doing so, achieving some degree of immortality. And while this is thought to be a recent whizz, in fact it goes well back in time. In 1953 J. Paul Getty gave a valuable Persian rug, the 'Coronation Carpet' and a Boucher tapestry to the Los Angeles Museum of Contemporary Art. That gift, said former Getty Museum curator Burton Fredericksen in *The Burdens of Wealth* (2015), 'may have come about primarily because of his need for deductions at a time when [Getty] found himself in higher tax brackets'.[43]

The tax aspect is far more complex than it might initially appear. It is time to look at the financial underpinnings of private museums: how these institutions are funded, how they are structured and whether they really are just a means of dodging tax.

3

Financing the Private Museum

If there's a moral, maybe it's this: don't start your own museum unless you're prepared to fund it in perpetuity.

William Poundstone, author, columnist[1]

In 2021, shortly after the death of its founder Sheldon Solow, the New York-based Solow Art and Architecture Foundation sold Sandro Botticelli's *Portrait of a Young Man Holding a Roundell* (*c.*1480) at Sotheby's. The depiction of a smooth-faced young man, holding a small portrait of a saint painted in the 14th century which had been inserted into the picture, was estimated at around $80 million. It had been consigned before Solow's death, and made $92.2 million with fees.[2]

Sheldon Solow, the real estate magnate who created the private operating foundation – a registered charity – paid about $1.3 million for the painting in 1982. By 2001, the work, now valued at $40.6 million, had been partially donated to the foundation. It was put on public view as a long-term loan to both the National Gallery of Art in Washington DC and the Metropolitan Museum of Art in New York. However other works of art in the foundation – by Matisse, Basquiat, Miró and Picasso, valued at some $200 million – were not accessible to the public, although they could be glimpsed through glass in Solow's building at 9 West 57th Street, just a block away from New York's Central Park.

After the sale at Sotheby's, the Solow Foundation saved at least $33 million in capital gains tax, since sales from such a foundation are tax-free. Solow himself, during his lifetime, was able to deduct the value of his art from his personal income taxes – up to 50 per cent – potentially saving, over the years, much more than the initial price of the portrait, and all of this quite legally. But it could be argued that the public purse lost out to a billionaire's crafty use of the US rules regulating private operating foundations, which under the US tax code are designated '501(c)(3) organisations'.

Following Solow's death in November 2020, his widow announced that the art still in the foundation would be turned into a private museum accessible to the public, affirming that this had been her late husband's intention all along.[3] At the time of writing, this had yet to happen. The case of the Solow Foundation is certainly one of the most egregious examples of what many criticise about private museums – that they are merely a vehicle for tax avoidance, and often a vanity project to boot.

In fact, the reality is far more complex. For a start, the tax avoidance aspect is largely confined to the United States; few other countries give tax breaks to citizens who start their own museums. An exception is the generous corporate philanthropy law in France (see below). Still, there are valid reasons to question the current state of affairs in the US – as did Senator Orrin Hatch in 2016. I will return to him later in this chapter.

Creating your own private museum is eye-wateringly expensive. A quick canter through the costliest ventures throws up examples around the world, but most notably in the United States. Among these are Glenstone, near Washington DC, where financier Mitchell Rales and his wife Emily built an extraordinarily beautiful gallery near their home. They donated $450 million in stock, between 2012 and 2014, to their foundation.[4] And they declared, on the foundation's tax form, a fair market value of its total assets at just over $1.8 billion in 2018.[5]

On the other side of the United States, in Los Angeles, real estate and insurance tycoon Eli Broad spent $140 million on the edifice for The Broad, without counting the art; in addition, Broad put a $200 million endowment into his foundation, to ensure its future.[6] In Europe, the luxury-goods magnate and Christie's owner François Pinault spent at least $225 million to redesign and install his three museums, again without counting running costs and the value of the art displayed in them.[7] In Paris, the Fondation Louis Vuitton cost an estimated €780 million in 2017, according to the French magazine *Marianne*. The building will pass into the hands of the city of Paris after 55 years, in 2062.[8]

But for the most enormous amount spent on a private museum, we must return to the US, to two museums. The first is Crystal Bridges Museum of American Art in Bentonville, Arkansas. Its founder is Alice Walton, daughter of Walmart founder Sam Walton, whose wealth totalled $64.7 billion in 2021, according to Forbes. She has spent hundreds of millions of dollars on art and on the building, to which a contemporary satellite, The Momentary, was added in 2020. The whole project cost, according to one commentator, around $1.6 billion to build and endow.[9]

The second is the massive museum under construction at the time of writing in Los Angeles, the creation of film director George Lucas. Cloud shaped, topped by a planted terrace and rising above more greenery, the building will show narrative art in many forms – from ancient art to contemporary cartoons, drawing on Lucas's 100,000-strong collection of everything from paintings, sculpture and photography to *Star Wars* ephemera. It reportedly cost $1 billion; in 2020 it had hired a chief curator and was slated to open in late 2021.[10]

Starting out

The initial funding for a private museum invariably comes from the art collector – or, in the case of corporate museums, the company. Collectors rarely start out intending to show their holdings to the public: an exception is the Chinese X Museum founder Michael Xufu Huang, who *started* by partnering in a museum – M WOODS in Beijing – at the age of just 20, and began collecting in earnest once he was involved in the institution.[11] This exception apart, art is generally initially collected for the home. But, at some point, most collectors move from accumulating in the home, finding themselves short of space to hang or even keep their collection, piling up works in storage, and finally taking the plunge and deciding to show to the public. In some cases, the owner's home becomes the exhibition space – the Boros Collection in Berlin, the Elliott Eyes Collection in Sydney and the Napoleone Collection in London, among many. This is a continuation of the tradition of the 'house museum' started in the 20th century by the likes of Isabella Stewart Gardner or Henry Huntington.

But the growing size of a collection, coupled with the various motivations outlined in the previous chapter, can lead either to a separate building being planned or an extension, separated from the living areas of the house. This, for instance, is the case with Glenstone or the Brant Foundation Art Study Center in Greenwich, Connecticut, established by publisher Peter Brant. He is a major player in the art market and has an extensive collection: two exhibitions a year of parts of it are held in a barn on the property adjoining Brant's home.

For the most deep-pocketed collector, a world-famous 'starchitect' might be tapped to build the new space, or a well-known designer brought in to transform an existing building. David Chipperfield, for example, designed the elegant Museo Jumex in Mexico City, and Herzog & de Meuron produced a minimalist linear building for the Goetz Collection in Munich.

When the collector decides to create a private museum, the choice of legal entity is often the first step. This will very much depend on the jurisdiction they are in, so the possibilities are extremely varied and not within the scope of this book to enumerate in detail. However, some sort of not-for-profit structure – often a foundation – is generally chosen, and this choice, notably in the US, can lead to founders radically reducing their tax exposure. The criticism I have most often heard of private museums is that such foundations allow owners to protect their wealth, diminish their tax obligations and reap the rewards of being seen as philanthropists. And even in countries without the favourable tax regime of the US, there is a strategy which consists of transferring the business costs into a foundation – the building, staffing and utility costs and so on – while keeping the art in the hands of the founders. This allows for eventual resale, something that is not possible once the collection itself is locked in a foundation.

While the laws in different jurisdictions vary, in order to achieve tax-exemption, there must be a demonstratable public benefit, through loans of the works of art in the foundation, grants and awards, an educational programme and public access. However, in the US, for example, all the expenses of the foundation as well as, say, a splashy launch party, would be tax deductible. Again, the criticism often aimed at this tax break is that this money diminishes the public purse, thus potentially reducing the amount that could be available for other publicly funded projects. The opposing argument is that the museums contribute to the cultural life of their area, help artists and offer outreach programmes and educational facilities that the state cannot or will not offer, and so are a net benefit for the community, particularly as public funding for arts education is being steadily eroded.

Establishing a charitable foundation is not that easy. In the UK, according to art lawyer James Carleton of Farrer & Co LLP in London:

> For an English charitable foundation, you need to register with and be accepted by the Charity Commission as well as HMRC. To achieve this, you must demonstrate that you are providing a 'public benefit' by preserving and maintaining a collection (or cultural asset), and, in the case of a private museum, you must grant public access to the items or asset owned by the foundation. In order to meet this requirement, you are thinking of at least 100 days opening: and you would likely have to be open during public holidays and weekends. This doesn't always suit owners and those setting up a charity: I do know of some who would like to fulfil this requirement by just being open during the weekdays and for a few weeks only! But that would just not be acceptable unless the collection or asset could be made available to the public on some other basis such as long-term loan.[12]

The rules vary between countries, particularly concerning tax breaks: the US has generous, some say too generous, provisions for those who establish private museums, while many countries – India, Indonesia and others – give no fiscal inducements at all. In China, as we shall see, the government tends to grant cheap land or otherwise facilitate the establishment of private museums. In some countries, the state does sometimes contribute to the costs of educational programmes or temporary exhibitions – for instance, the exhibitions of Philippe Méaille's collection at the Château de Montsoreau in France, or of Lu Xun's at the Sifang Art Museum in China – but these are mainly exceptions. Méaille holds the world's biggest collection of works by the artist collective Art & Language, which he shows in a chateau in the Loire region, receiving state funding for his temporary exhibitions. As for Lu, his collection ranges from architectural commissions to performance pieces. While mainly self-financed, the Sifang museum does also receive 'a small amount' of money from government sources for specific projects.[13]

The United States: 501(c)(3) organisations and the Hatch Report

There is no doubt that the US system of tax exemption has drawn the most ire. Never one to hold back, the New York-based writer, artist and teacher Kenny Schachter is scathing: 'Private museums only make sense under one condition, that there is no public institution within a 75-mile radius!' he griped, before continuing: 'The Broad [in Los Angeles] should really be called an auction house evening sale museum – it shows obvious things by obvious people – but it does not fulfil the role of a museum.' Speaking before the death of Eli Broad in 2021, he added:

> Los Angeles museums have been spending decades building a constituency with dwindling financial support for their activities . . . and then people such as Eli Broad open their own museums . . . I don't say he's badly intentioned but he's having

> a tax write-off for his folly – it's nothing more than a folly, it's disgraceful that that money won't go to public museums. The Rales are the same, they call it a museum and open up with the bare minimum prerequisite educational purposes and visitation rights and then they get a complete 100 per cent tax write off![14]

Indeed, when the Rales donated $450 million in stock to their foundation in Washington DC, they paid no capital gains tax at all.[15] On the other hand, they no longer have the art, which must stay in the foundation. The question then to be asked is whether the public benefit is enough to justify the loss to the public purse? It is difficult to find a clear answer.

According to British writer Paul Vallely, philanthropy today tends to favour elitist causes – 'A lot goes to the arts, sports teams and other cultural pursuits' – as well as the elite universities that the givers themselves attended. 'The wealthy, when they do give, largely direct their money to sectors from which they benefit themselves,' he writes.[16] And yet many private museums do make enormous efforts to engage new audiences and appeal to a more diverse audience. Jupiter Artland near Edinburgh, for example, is only open to school groups in the winter and will even pay for the buses when schools cannot afford them.

In the US, there are two sorts of tax-exempt charitable organisations classified as a '501(c)(3)'. One is a public charity and receives its funding from the public and the government. The other concerns us here: the private foundation or, more precisely, the private operating foundation. Set up for charitable or educational reasons, the organisation must make its tax filings available publicly[17] as part of its tax-exempt status and fulfil other requirements aimed, for example, at preventing self-dealing or paying salaries over a fair market rate.

Provided the owner has owned the work of art that they donate to a foundation for over a year, they will be able to deduct between 30 per cent and 50 per cent from their adjusted gross income.[18] The fair market value of the work of art is assessed by the Inland Revenue

Service (IRS) at the time of the donation. For example, a $1 million Warhol donated to a private foundation could potentially save a considerable amount on the donor's income tax bill. But, of course, the owner no longer has the Warhol and, once in the foundation, it cannot be resold.

There is another way, though, of optimising tax: loaning to a foundation. If the owner thinks the art might appreciate in value, they might start by making it a loan or only a partial gift, which could be renewable for five years. By then, the value of the work of art could have gone up, resulting in a greater tax deduction. Should the foundation be dissolved – a rare occurrence – the assets, including the art, would have to be donated to another 501(c)(3) organisation; they cannot be returned to the donor/founder/successor for resale.

Not all collectors are motivated by tax incentives, however. For example, in Texas the renowned collector and philanthropist Howard Rachofsky tells me: 'There is a fine line with private foundations.' He shows his and his wife Cindy's collection in a building called The Warehouse in Dallas, Texas, part of his larger foundation, The Rachofsky House: 'I think some are used as a tax shelter. I want to be clear, we don't do that. We don't take a paperclip out of the Warehouse! And it's easier, all the same, to follow the rules and moral code than to find a way around them.'[19]

The Hatch Report

In 2016 a Senate committee on finance investigated several such foundations and issued a highly critical report. Initiated by Senator Orrin Hatch, the report singled out 11 private, not-for-profit foundations and found that, in some, the short visiting hours, locations close to the founders' homes, poor advertising, governance and other elements could be problematic. 'I remain concerned that this area of our tax code is ripe for exploitation,' Hatch had written in a letter to the IRS.[20]

Despite this, the tax code wasn't modified. The tax specialist and Global Head of Art Law at Withers Bergman LLP, Diana Wierbicki, told me: 'After the 2016 Hatch Report we waited to see if the IRS would make changes. While this has not happened, it has probably made founding donors and boards more mindful about closer scrutiny.'[21] And as the art-related financial advisor Doug Woodham noted: 'Public scrutiny is a good disinfectant, and the Hatch Report certainly had the effect of making some of these private museums change their behaviour.'[22]

The question that could be asked is why very wealthy people, who can certainly afford to be philanthropic and indeed have a genuine concern for the community, can be so keen to squeeze every advantage out of their generosity. According to curator and former museum director Maxwell Anderson: 'I know so many millionaires who have grocery card plastic tabs on their keyrings so they can get a little discount. You cannot overestimate the degree of concern about safeguarding wealth – I think people become more concerned about eliminating the tax burden the wealthier they get.'[23] And to be fair, since the US tax laws allow all sorts of deductions for private museums, it is inevitable that owners will make use of them.

A final tax aspect which may well have stimulated the creation of private museums was, again in the US, the ending of an attractive incentive for 'partial gifts', which had allowed owners to legally 'donate' works to museums in increments over the years but keep them in their own homes. As the art appreciated in value, so did the level of the tax deduction. This came to an end in 2006 when, despite an outcry from museums and collectors, the law was modified. 'The law was changed in three ways,' explains Doug Woodham: 'The fair market value of the work became fixed at the time of the donation; the donation had to be completed in ten years, and the work had to go on show in the museum for a period corresponding to the percentage gifted.' This is thought to have triggered the establishment of some private museums in the US, since owners no longer benefited from this tax break and so decided to create their own art spaces.

French corporate philanthropy

France has a generous corporate philanthropy law, which enables a company to deduct 60 per cent of the amount it gives to cultural projects from its corporate tax bill. Dubbed the 'Aillagon Law' – after a former Minister of Culture and close collaborator of François Pinault – the regulation allowed Bernard Arnault's Fondation Louis Vuitton to cut its tax by a whopping €581.1 million over an 11-year period.[24] While the foundation is an undisputed cultural benefit for Paris – and the city will gain possession of its building in 2062 – the fact is that the state largely paid for the project.

As for the commercial benefits the formidable luxury-goods company derives from having such a prominent platform, these are more difficult to assess. But they must be attractive, as other companies in France have taken note: a report by the *Cour des Comptes,* which examines public spending, noted that the number of companies taking advantage of the law leapt from 6500 in 2005 to 68,930 in 2017.[25]

Interestingly, Arnault's great rival François Pinault did not take any tax breaks for his third museum, the Bourse du Commerce project – it is totally financed by his family. Speaking on the radio station France Culture, he said: 'I didn't want people to say that the state was financing my little artistic whims, while others are starving. Should it be the state's priority to finance private foundations? Art is important, but some things are even more important.'[26]

Running costs

Setting aside for the moment the tax incentives, the cost of running a museum is inevitably difficult to quantify, but the *Private Art Museum Report* had this to say in 2016: 'It is estimated that, on average, operating one square meter of museum costs $431 worth of expenses per year. Given that the average size of a private museum is 3,389 m^2, this signifies that the average private museum's yearly operating costs come to a total of $1.5 million.'[27] Statements such as this may give an idea of average running costs, but the specifics are far more complicated, depending on the size of the museum, its ambitions and its location. In California, The Broad's yearly expenses in 2018 were just over $15.6 million, according to that year's tax filing. At the other end of the spectrum, a small 'house' museum may cost comparatively little, since expenses are integrated into the owner's personal budget.

'Collectors are incredibly naïve about costs,' says a public museum director, speaking off the record:

> For example, when David Walsh started working on the project to build the Museum of Old and New Art in Tasmania, his first idea was it would cost Aus$2 million a year (about US$1.3 million) to run. We said it was more likely to cost AUS$8 million–AUS$10 million. And Walsh first thought he could run it with four staff; he had no idea about research or even the logistics of putting a show together.[28]

Founding a museum is one thing but sustaining it financially into the future is another. As we have seen, collectors frequently underestimate the costs of keeping a museum going, and indeed some do fall by the wayside, generally because funding becomes an issue. In some cases, it becomes apparent even during the lifetime of the founder that the project is unsustainable. In others, the passage to the following generation brings the project to an end. This will be examined in Chapter 6.

The impact of the pandemic

And then there was the 2020–21 pandemic. In 2020 an alarming statement from UNESCO warned that 13 per cent of museums worldwide might never reopen their doors after the crisis.[29] Across the world, many galleries and museums were closed for around a year, leaving them with sometimes unsustainable losses. The closures obliterated ticket, gift-shop, catering, event-rental and other income; even during the partial reopening in autumn 2020, museums saw far fewer visitors, thereby increasing losses.[30]

In June 2020 the American Alliance of Museums (AAM) published a report based on a survey of 760 of its members. One third of museum directors said that their establishments could close forever, if no outside assistance became available; and 56 per cent said that they had less than six months' worth of funds to cover operations. This could mean, said the AAM, that 12,000 museums could potentially close.[31] The renowned Metropolitan Museum of Art in New York said in August 2020 that it expected a budget shortfall of as much as $150 million for the current and the next fiscal year, and that it had laid off 81 staff.[32] In June 2020 the non-profit Americans for the Arts organisation estimated losses in the US arts sector at $6.7 billion. Job losses were rife, across the world.

Even when museums reopened, visitor numbers were a fraction of previous levels, inevitably impacting on their budgets. *The Art Newspaper*'s annual visitor numbers survey, published in March 2021, showed that overall attendance at the 100 most visited museums in 2020 dropped by a staggering 77 per cent – and among these were private institutions such as UCCA in Beijing (down 48 per cent), Crystal Bridges in Bentonville (down 50 per cent), Soumaya in Mexico City (down 71 per cent) and the Museu Coleção Berardo in Lisbon (down 70 per cent). Nevertheless, the situation for private museums was different, since their survival was dependent on the pockets of the founders; in addition, some such as The Broad, were free to visit and therefore not dependent on ticket sales. However, with lower footfall, the income from the shop and cafes was likely to plummet.

At the time of time of writing it was difficult to say how this situation would play out, since the impact of the 2020–21 pandemic is yet to be fully measured. However, it seems inevitable that owners of private spaces might decide to take similar measures to public institutions, by slimming down head counts and reducing the number of their exhibitions, extending their duration. What's more, exhibitions attracting mass crowds are likely to be put on hold for a while and it is only over the next few years that the impact of the pandemic on private art museums will start to become clear, with their fate inevitably tied up with the fortunes of their founders. An encouraging sign is that, in 2021, the number of billionaires in the world was 2755, with a total worth of $13.1 trillion, and a staggering 86 per cent of them were richer than the year before.[33] While not all by any means had established private museums, more and more certainly have the resources to do so.

4

The Proliferation of Private Museums in China

Traditionally, the Chinese have always been collectors. After the hiatus in the 20th century, when the Cultural Revolution and Great Leap Forward made collecting impossible, those who have been able to accumulate wealth recently may well use some of their money to buy art.

Rebecca Wei, Lévy Gorvy; former chair, Christie's Asia[1]

Much has been written about a building 'frenzy' of private museums in China, with some hair-raising figures bandied about. Back in 2014, *The Economist* declared that one new private museum a day was being opened.[2] According to Grace Ai, Deputy Secretary General of the China Museums Association: 'The total number of Chinese museums was just 2000 in the year 2000; in 2019 it was 5535.' Collectively, they attracted 1.2 billion visitors in 2019, she says.[3]

Here China is playing catch-up with the West; just 25 museums existed in China in 1949 and many of those fell into ruin during the Cultural Revolution. But according to the 13th Five-Year Plan (2016–20), one museum on average was being built every two days, meaning that there is now one per 250,000 people. And, according to Ai, the plan is to build more museums, both public and private. China is putting its money where its mouth is: since 2008, the state has invested $441 million annually to give free admission to museums, and 4743 of these Chinese institutions do indeed have no admission fees. As for the 1710 private museums, these generally charge for entry. However, the number of those showing modern and contemporary art – the focus of this book – is much smaller: between 200 and 300, according to author Shaun Wang, writing in 2017.[4]

Encouraging cultural initiatives is all part of this governmental 'soft power' strategy. 'Non-state museums are an important part of the museum system of our country,' continues Ai. 'The development of non-state museums is conducive to optimizing the museum system . . . filling the gaps in the different categories . . . and stimulating social vitality.' The Chinese government grants low rental and government subsidies to private museum owners. A spokesperson for Wang Wei (co-founder of the three Long Museums, two in Shanghai, one in Chongqing) was not able to say exactly how much the government subsidies were: 'They vary greatly every year,' she said, but pointed out that the most important source of funding was from Wang Wei and her husband Liu Yiqian, followed by government aid for cultural development.[5]

According to Rebecca Wei, this represented somewhere between 10 and 30 per cent of the cost of the museums. Helping the establishment of private museums is part of the government aim to boost the tally of cultural institutions, although it was partially disrupted by the COVID-19 pandemic. Some openings were delayed, including the He Art Museum in Shunde, while the Star museum in Shanghai was postponed to an unspecified date.[6]

Complicating the issue is the fact that many of China's new museums are 'white elephants' with weak collections, poor governance and unsatisfactory conservation conditions. 'A lot of China's contemporary art museums are very small and really don't move the needle,' says Rebecca Wei. 'The owners can buy highlights but that doesn't mean the museums are significant compared to overseas museums,' she adds. However, Wei underlines that the Chinese have always been collectors, and once collecting became possible again, those who have amassed wealth have often used some of their money to buy art.

Budiardjo 'Budi' Tek, founder of the Yuz Museum Shanghai, concurs: 'Many of the so-called "private museums" are actually just exhibition halls,' he told *Artnet* in 2019. 'One day in the future – maybe in another five, ten years – they might start to realize that museums need to have collections, and then they'll understand the necessity of having good artworks. But today, if you are talking about 1500 museums, maybe only a few dozen have actual collections.'[7]

So why are Chinese collectors founding their own museums? The first reason is simple: sheer wealth. The increase in fortune for some in China is massive; the total wealth of the 400 members of the China Rich List rose to $1.55 trillion between 2019 and 2020, according to Forbes.[8] And while some of those fortunes were dented by the 2020–21 pandemic, they have not been eliminated, by any means. As an example, in June 2020 an unidentified Chinese online bidder chased Francis Bacon's *Triptych Inspired by the Oresteia of Aeschylus* (1981), going almost all the way to the final price of $84.55 million – although eventually losing out to a Sotheby's specialist on behalf of an unidentified bidder. This wealth may be openly flaunted, as by the couple Wang Wei and Liu Yiqian with their three Long museums. Liu Yiqian, the taxi-driver-turned-billionaire, has used social media to brag about his high-priced purchases, including Amedeo Modigliani's *Nu Couché* (1917–18) for $170.4 million in 2015.[9] However, his case is exceptional and many private museum founders are more discreet in their collecting, even when they do build smart new museums.

Along with the growth in personal wealth, the booming art market for Chinese contemporary art, notably around 2010–11, was an additional trigger for collecting and for opening a museum. With prices skyrocketing, owners saw art as a solid investment. 'The more you are able to control and show your own collection the more opportunity [there is] for that collection to gain in value, so you are also controlling that market with your own collection,' said Jeffrey Johnson, Director of Columbia University's China Megacities Lab in 2016.[10] In addition, there is a long tradition in Asia for buyers to favour tangible investments – gold, real estate or art – over stocks and shares, which are perceived as less 'safe'.

Contemporary art – a hot potato?

On my past trips to China, I have sometimes heard from contacts there that the Chinese government encourages private individuals to set up their own museums of contemporary art, rather than doing so itself, because of the potentially controversial nature of contemporary art. Such art may explore uncomfortable themes and be difficult to control, and so not play into the government-sanctioned role of museums in preserving historical artefacts, instilling national pride and educating its citizens in their cultural heritage, as well as offering a positive view of the country.

Rebecca Wei notes: 'Contemporary art had more controversial content in the 1980s and 1990s, but now, if the state encourages private collectors to build their own spaces, it's rather because state-owned museums don't have the money [to buy and display contemporary art].' And she adds that the lack of tax breaks means that there is no incentive for private collectors to give to state museums. Another reason, common to other countries, is that collectors fear losing control of their art, something that is even more acute in mainland China. In this context it is worth noting that in 2012 the Swiss collector Uli Sigg decided not to give his remarkable collection of Chinese art to a mainland institution for this reason, fearing that 'the heavy hand of state censorship would prevent many of the works from being shown'.[11] It went instead to Hong Kong, for the projected M+ Museum.

Unfortunately, by 2020, Hong Kong was also seeing increasing control from the mainland authorities after a new security law was imposed, to widespread protest but also widespread crushing of dissent. Asked about this, Sigg claimed that this would not affect the museum: 'I have very strong commitments from the chairman [of West Kowloon Cultural District, where M+ is located], the director of the museum, the CEO – each and every one of them has expressed the strongest intent to preserve the current status in this respect and not allow any restraints,' he said in 2020.[12] However, in March 2021, Henry Tang Ying-yen, Chairman of the West Kowloon Cultural District Authority, said that the arts district 'will definitely uphold the law, comply with the Basic Law, local laws, and the national security law'.[13] And this meant, for instance, that the museum would not display Ai Weiwei's *Study of Perspective: Tiananmen Square* (1997), a photograph of the artist raising his middle finger in front of Tiananmen Square in Beijing.

The real estate connection – and other motivations

It is impossible to ignore the importance of real estate in this context and, while this pattern – of developers being the founders of private museums – is common around the world, it is often key in China. 'Initially, the museum becomes a unique selling point for real estate. Afterward, the museum brands the enterprise in the direction of an "artistic life". Lastly, the museum allows the enterprise to work towards the role of public welfare,' says Zhao Qie, Director of the Times Museum Guangzhou.[14] Going even further, Lao Li, former Director of the Songzhuang Art Museum in an artists' village on the east side of Beijing, says: 'Constructing a museum is only a real estate strategy in disguised form.'[15]

By offering such a 'cultural industry' facility, the developers can get cheap land and even sometimes the status of 'duty-free storage zones' which can be used to promote the whole project. Then the museum itself can be allowed to wither once the other objectives have been fulfilled – they can become 'mosquito museums', an empty shell only useful for housing mosquitos, according to Zhang Lin, CEO of the Shanghai Museum of Glass.[16]

Other private museums are not just real estate or vanity projects. In 2018 I visited the new A4 Art Museum outside Chengdu – one of China's second-tier cities, with a population of 14 million. A4 forms part of a vast new town, Luxelakes, with an artificial lake, housing, shops, restaurants and so on, linked to Chengdu by two new underground stations. The museum itself is tucked into a Brutalist building that also houses the sales office for the area, and yet the institution has a real programme, holds exhibitions and conferences, is planning artists' residencies and has worked with the Yokohama Museum of Art and the Kyoto Art Center in Japan. It adds a cultural attraction to what would be otherwise a rather sterile suburban housing development. And it plays into another advantage: in China, art is perceived to be cool, hip and a lifestyle choice. Offering art is a powerful way of boosting the attraction of a project and at the same time offering an 'experience'. This is taken to its logical conclusion elsewhere in China by the K11 malls, luxury shopping buildings which feature a museum as an additional incentive to bring in visitors.

The other less-than-philanthropic reason for starting a museum is the hope that the works displayed will gain in value. Again, this is reflected in other parts of the world, but perhaps even more so in China where the investment aspect is extremely important. I have often heard unverifiable reports that some owners use their museums to buy works of art at the 25 per cent 'museum discount' and then resell at full price.[17] Other museums are little short of shops. This is reinforced by the blurring of luxury goods with art, with, for instance, the Museum of Contemporary Art in Shanghai having held exhibitions of Dior, Ferragamo, Chanel and Van Cleef and Arpels, or the Bulgari exhibition at Shanghai's Aurora Museum.

The three 'waves' of Chinese museum building

As we have seen, contemporary art museums are very recent arrivals on the Chinese scene but, even then, there have been three phases in their development. The first private museum to be opened to the public was in 1991, the Yang Huang in Beijing, and a number followed before the early years of the 21st century. However, many closed down quickly, lacking a solid management structure (examples include the Upriver Gallery in Chengdu, Dongyu museum in Shenyang and Taida Dangdai

Art Museum in Tianjin). 'This first-generation model was essentially about storage,' says Rebecca Wei:

> When the owner ran out of space for the collection, he opened it as a museum. For all the early private museums, the main function was storage and display – some didn't even have any curators, education programmes and so on. But the owners found to their shock that it was immensely costly to run them, which was one reason why many closed.

During the early years of the 21st century there was a second wave, ushered in by the inauguration in 2007 of the Ullens Center for Contemporary Art (now UCCA) in Beijing's 798 art zone. It was founded by the Belgian collector Guy Ullens, who had made his fortune in the food industry. Ullens had a collection of Chinese art but, according to his former curator and an outspoken critic, Fei Dawei, he reversed his initial intention to make the centre non-profit and a philanthropic contribution to Chinese art. 'Many of Ullens's commitments were followed by major changes, which calls into question his honesty,' Fei said in one interview.[18]

Ullens was accused of wanting to make money from the centre, and for years he searched for a buyer while gradually selling most of his holdings of Chinese art.[19] In 2017 a group of private investors restructured UCCA and put it on a solid footing, retaining the respected academic and curator Philip Tinari, who was already at the helm. UCCA now has two more spaces. One is Dune, an environmentally friendly building tunnelled under a sand dune in the resort beach town of Beidaihe in Hebei province, 300 km from Beijing. The project was funded by one of UCCA's partners, Aranya, and calls itself an 'innovative art vacation destination' – yet another indication of how, in China, art and lifestyle are often intimately connected. The other is UCCA Edge, which opened in Shanghai in spring 2021.

Among the other museums created during that second phase are the Today Art Museum in Beijing, another one born of the real estate industry, and the OCAT group's four museums in Beijing, Shenzhen, Xi'an and Shanghai, once again linked to real estate.

The strongest building wave was the third phase, which started after the 2007–08 global financial crisis and saw dozens of new museums being opened: Shanghai Minsheng Art Museum, K11 in Hong Kong, Rockbund Art Museum in Shanghai, the three Long Museums, Yuz Museum Shanghai, Sifang Art Museum in Nanjing and many more. By this time there was better awareness of issues of structuring, governance, curation, budgeting and so on. But the model of an excessively interventionist owner can also be an issue, as elsewhere in the world. 'The second generation [of young Chinese collectors] is far more sophisticated, they have been educated abroad, they are bilingual and often have majored in art,' says Rebecca Wei, who cites the He, Sifang and Long museums as institutions where the second generation is either involved in the operation already or will eventually take over.

There is certainly some way to go for certain of China's museums. I visited two of the Long museums and found neither particularly 'user friendly' and both rather deserted. There was little information available and, notably, the West Bund one, housed in a former factory, is a dispiriting experience with massive dull grey concrete walls and gigantic spaces which do little to enhance any art on show. 'A lot of these private museums do not have a foundation, people who understand art and running a museum. I think the private museums are pretty chaotic. Lots of them do not have a good model and so it is hard for them to advance,' says Rebecca Catching, who worked in Shanghai as a curator between 2001 and 2016.[20] She accuses some of 'incompetent waffling leadership, no funding strategy, a lack of transparency, no respect for curatorial knowledge, or even basic issues such as budgeting and prompt payment of suppliers'. And she also criticises the lack of managerial experience: 'Hiring is skewed by *guanxi* [personal contacts] networks. In one case close to 40 per cent of the curatorial staff had personal family connections – many of them were blood relations,' she said.

Public-private partnerships in China

These criticisms do not apply to all private museums in China, by any means. Widely admired is the Rockbund museum in Shanghai. A particular case also in Shanghai is the Yuz Museum, housed in a former airplane hangar in the West Bund area of the city. Its founder, the Indonesian-Chinese collector Budiardjo 'Budi' Tek made his fortune in poultry production and is sometimes dubbed the 'chicken king'. He started a museum in Jakarta in 2004 and eventually acquired some 1500 large-scale works, by both Chinese and international artists. In 2014 he opened the Yuz. Perhaps its most notable show was the excellent 2016 retrospective of Alberto Giacometti, curated by the Giacometti Foundation's director, Catherine Grenier, and held in collaboration with the artist's Parisian foundation.[21] The previous year, Yuz hosted the highly popular *Rain Room* by Random International, drawing queues around the block.[22]

Struck by pancreatic cancer, Tek's plans to extend into Bali with a museum-cum-real estate operation were cancelled, and an attempt to preserve the collection by turning it into a public entity fell flat, because there was no legal framework to do so in China. So he explored a deal with the Los Angeles County Museum of Art (LACMA) to turn Yuz into a public institution. This would be achieved by transferring ownership of the collection – or part of it, as the family would inherit some, on Tek's death – to a public foundation.[23] However, this project, at the time of writing, did not appear to be completed; repeated emails to LACMA asking for more information on the subject were left unanswered.

While Tek, motivated by his health issues, is attempting to solve the question of what will happen to his collection after his death, most private Chinese museums are not doing so. According to one source, a possible outcome is that as the contracts for hiring the land run out, the institutions could gradually be brought back under government administration, possibly branded with the founders' names. This, said the source, would tie in with the increasingly authoritarian regime under China's President for life, Xi Jinping.[24]

Meanwhile there have been a few international partnerships, such as that of the Centre Pompidou and West Bund Museum in Shanghai, in which the local Xuhui government partnered with the French institution in 2019, paying about €2.7 million a year for a five-year contract to exhibit works. The Pompidou is completely responsible for programming and the works are displayed in the David Chipperfield-designed West Bund Museum building. Hit by the pandemic, its footfall was weak – 370,000 in 2020 – and it was criticised for 'lack of a clear identity, weak shows and awkward design' in the French *Quotidien de l'Art*, although the Centre Pompidou president Serge Lasvignes was quoted as saying time would tell if it had 'been useful'.[25] Another such partnership was in Shenzhen, in 2017, where London's Victoria and Albert Museum opened a new design gallery in a large-scale retail, commercial and residential development. It was supposed to be the 'cultural heart' of the project and, again, the initial proposal was for five years; in November 2019 it was extended to 2024.

The interest for the French or British museums in such partnerships is obvious – a way to extend their mission and brand, bringing (hopefully) more visitors into the 'mothership' as Chinese tourism continues to expand. It is too early to say how these initiatives will evolve, post-pandemic, with the severe drop in Chinese tourism to the West.

5

From Private to Public – Partnerships

Sooner or later most private museums cannot survive without state intervention.

Chris Dercon, in *The Private Museum of the Future* (2018)[1]

Virtually all public museums started as private collections – from the French royal holdings which eventually went into the Louvre or the wealthy antiquary Elias Ashmole who gifted his collection to Oxford University. In 1683 the Ashmolean Museum opened in Oxford as Britain's first public museum and the world's first university museum. Sir Hans Sloane's bequest led to the foundation of the British Museum in 1753; the Medici collection in Florence, Italy, became the Uffizi in the 1830s.

Public museums have always relied on private collectors, both for their initial inventories and for subsequent support, even in countries where there is also governmental funding. In the United States, where state funding for museums is minimal, private philanthropy is fundamental to their very existence. Traditionally, and not only in the US, donors have helped public museums with loans, gifts and bequests of art, as well as funding. Wealthy patrons sit on museum boards, exchanging their expertise in other fields (for example, finance) and supporting the institutions with hard cash. Their reward may well include receiving help from the museum's curators in constituting their own collection, quite apart from the prestige and pleasure of supporting the institution.

Museums have every interest in giving that advice, in the hope of someday reaping the benefit through bequests. For example, the New York-based patron and philanthropist Agnes Gund – past president of the Museum of Modern Art (MoMA) and on many boards, including the Cleveland Museum of Art – told me: 'I collect mainly for museums today, so it's rather what *they* want rather than what *I* would want.' Most of her collection is promised to various museums after her death.[2]

This form of patronage, however, has been upended by the advent of private museums in the 21st century. As we have seen, instead of bequeathing their collections to a museum, collectors are opening their own. Their motivations, as outlined in Chapter 2, include the desire to control their collection and keep it together beyond their lifetime, a distrust of state institutions, and the glory and visibility of having one's own art space and so leaving a legacy.

There is also a feeling among some collectors that today's museums are too staid, notably in the field of contemporary art. '[Public museums] have been slow to diversify, in the artists they collect, in the people they hire. They've been slow respond to new technologies, to embrace performance, technology, moving image,' says cultural consultant András Szántó.[3] Similarly, the Miami-based collector Rosa de la Cruz told Marta Gnyp for her 2016 book *The Shift*: 'I think that the [public] museums can't move fast enough. The whole framework of the museum is so bureaucratic and slow that in today's world they just stay behind because there is no life in those museums. Contemporary collectors can move fast though. They don't have to confer with a group of people that have to agree.'[4]

The public-private model

There is widespread cooperation between the public and private sectors already. This may consist of private collectors lending to public institutions – for example, the Whitechapel Gallery in London has shown selections from the Fondazione Sandretto Re Rebaudengo collection[5] and hosted the V-A-C Live film programme, initiated by the Russian foundation backed by Leonid Mikhelson.[6] And in California, in 2017, Pacific Standard Time was a much lauded, state-wide initiative bringing together arts organisations of all types.[7]

Another model exists, however, that has seen private collectors establish more permanent and complex relationships with public museums, with the collector lending a collection and the institution, local municipality or the state picking up the tab. In theory this should be a win-win situation: the institution gains works that it could not afford to buy; the collector sees the holdings conserved, insured and displayed at no cost to them, plus accruing plaudits for their public-spiritedness and generosity.[8] And it should be mentioned that exhibition in a public art space tends to boost the value of the art or collection, something that owners are generally perfectly aware of, even if it is not their primary motivation.

Some of these arrangements have worked very well; others have proved more problematic. In Germany, the Museum Brandhorst in Munich was opened in 2009 in a custom-built edifice, entirely funded by the state of Bavaria, to display 20th- and 21st-century paintings, sculptures and installations – including 100 works by Andy Warhol and 60 by Cy Twombly, as well as pieces by Damien Hirst, Joseph Beuys and Jean-Michel Basquiat – from the collection of Udo Brandhorst, whose late wife Annette was heiress to the Henkel chemical and consumer goods giant. Bavaria also paid an undisclosed sum to Brandhorst in a partial acquisition of the collection and in return he contributed €120 million towards the museum's endowment fund. In 2018, according to Georgina Walker, the Brandhorst's annual acquisition budget of €2 million exceeded that of all state-operated museums in Bavaria, leading to her reflection that the 'significant amount of money' spent on the Brandhorst might have been better spread between other museums in the area.[9] And Brandhorst received tax benefits and the prestige of having a museum in his own name – which remains publicly funded and operated.

There are other examples. In 2014 Ingvild Goetz donated 375 works of art from her 5000-strong collection – along with the Herzog & de Meuron building created to house them – to the state of Bavaria. Her collection spans Arte Povera and American painting to media art, and features artists such as Rosemarie Trockel, Thomas Schütte, Mike Kelley and Peter Fischli/David Weiss. Apart from the 375 donated works, the rest of the collection is on loan, for an initial period of ten years; the state of Bavaria, meanwhile, now picks up the bill for everything – the operation of the museum, staffing and so on. However, Goetz retains control, curates the exhibitions and arranges loans to other establishments as well as adding to the collection, the bulk of which remains her property and could, in theory, be withdrawn, although this seems highly improbable. This situation could be interpreted as a win-win, as Munich got a fine collection for nothing, but of course does have to pay the running costs for a museum over which it does not have total control.

Such arrangements can also be subject to reversal, illustrating their sometimes fragile nature. In a 'painful' end to a loan agreement, Berlin's state museums announced in 2020 that the collector Friedrich Christian Flick, heir to an industrial fortune, was withdrawing 1500 works of modern and contemporary art which had been loaned to the museums. He had also financed the €7.5 million refit of the Rieckhallen to exhibit the collection.[10]

As we have seen, maintaining control over a collection is often the founder's prime consideration, and some cases have seen failed attempts to cut deals with state or local authorities, whereby costs would be borne by the state but the collector would remain free to buy and sell at will. An example was Charles Saatchi's plan to donate his gallery to the British public in 2010; he proposed to give his prized array of works by Young British Artists – the movement he was fundamental in launching – and £25 million to establish a museum. However, talks with Arts Council England broke down, notably because Saatchi reportedly had planned to part-finance the new museum by being allowed to buy and sell items in the permanent collection – something banned by the

UK's Museums' Association.[11] Saatchi finally opened his own gallery in London's smart Chelsea district in 2008 and initially hosted exhibitions from his own collections. However, his increasing disengagement from art collecting, and personal issues including a divorce, led to the building morphing away from an exhibition space for his holdings and towards a 'for hire' model hosting art fairs, gala events and exhibitions such as *Tutankhamun*[12] or a Rolling Stones extravaganza in 2016.[13]

While partnerships with public institutions would seem to be the ideal way to benefit both the public – giving access to otherwise hidden-away works of art – and the collector, who has their treasures looked after, it can also be a way of increasing the value of a collector's holdings on the open market. The institutions are caught in a dilemma; by accepting a collection on loan, they increase the richness of their holdings, notably in works they could never afford to buy. However, they also run the risk of being 'used' by some collectors.

An example is that of Hans Grothe, a German construction magnate who lent some of his holdings of major post-1960s German artists, including Joseph Beuys, Gerhard Richter, Thomas Demand, Andreas Gursky and Thomas Ruff, to the local authority in Duisburg. Grothe agreed to donate 130 works to the city and accepted a $19-million grant towards the creation of a private 'Grothe Museum' to display his collection, sited on the city's inland harbour. But in 2019 Grothe sold 700 works from his collection to Wella haircare billionaires Sylvia and Ulrich Ströher for a stunning €50 million. The museum was renamed MKM Museum Küppersmühle für Moderne Kunst after the Ströhers took on Grothe's obligations.[14]

To return to the opening of this chapter, however, bequests to public institutions fortunately have not entirely disappeared from the landscape.

The Rachofsky Warehouse

A remarkable story comes from Dallas, Texas, where collectors Cindy and Howard Rachofsky, together with two other couples, pledged their collections to the Dallas Museum of Art in 2005 in what, at the time, was a $245-million gift – now probably worth four or five times that amount, according to Rachofsky.[15] The pledge includes masterworks by artists such as Matthew Barney, Joseph Beuys, Louise Bourgeois, Vija Celmins, Philip Guston, Jasper Johns, Donald Judd, Ellsworth Kelly, Franz Kline, Willem de Kooning, Jackson Pollock, Sol LeWitt, Bruce Nauman, Sigmar Polke, Gerhard Richter, Mark Rothko, Robert Ryman and Richard Tuttle. In addition, the 800-strong Rachofsky collection has extensive strengths in American Minimalism, post-war Italian art, Arte Povera, Gutai, Mono-ha and Dansaekhwa; the gifts will be absolutely transformative for the museum.

Howard Rachofsky explains:

> Cindy and I have built our collection over 30 to 40 years, and the relationship with the museum which led to the proposed gift dates to over 16 years ago. The pledge was initiated by our friends Marguerite and the late Robert Hoffman, along with Deedie and the late Rusty Rose. We decided that, as opposed to waiting until we are old or dead, we would make a pre-emptive move because of our long-standing relationship with the museum. The way the gift works, whatever is in the respective collections at the time of death will go to the museum after paying the various debts or obligations. This way it provides for additional acquisitions or deaccessions. So it will build out the museum's holdings.

An exhibition was held at the museum in 2007, curated by María de Corral, to show what the museum will look like in the future once the pledges have been fulfilled; it is documented in the book *Fast Forward*.[16]

'The theory behind the pledge was to continue to participate in the process of helping to develop the museum collection,' says Rachofsky. 'We don't act as curators per se but we are helping in an informal advisory role.' And they have indeed continued to make gifts, including discussing leaving The Warehouse, the large space which shows the

Rachofsky Collection, to the museum, although that decision and the details had not been finalised at time of writing.

The Rachovskys and their friends are a reminder of an earlier model of philanthropy, when collectors left their art to enrich their local museums, but one that is rarer today. In the next chapter we will look at the sustainability and legacy of private museums and why, in some cases, things go wrong.

6

Legacy, Sustainability and Why Private Museums Sometimes Die

I wouldn't be surprised if half of these private museums disappear after the death of the founder. But does that necessarily matter? New ones are being created all the time.

Martin Bailey, writer and Van Gogh specialist[1]

The survival of a private museum beyond the lifetime of the founder can be extremely problematic. Creating a place to store and display what may be a carefully built-up collection, over decades, is easier than ensuring its long-term sustainability. 'There are a huge number of people who built their own museums and never thought about the sustainability of the project. How can you forget something so simple?' asks cultural consultant Sébastien Montabonel.[2]

The obvious first issue is long-term funding. Collectors' successors may not look kindly on what may well be a money pit when, in the absence of an endowment, they will have to pick up the bills. As we have seen, running a museum can be extremely expensive, and successors' interests may lie elsewhere. But there are further reasons why the future of many private museums is problematic. Returning to the question of successors, the private museums I cover in this book are all devoted to modern and contemporary art, and the next generation often does not have the same tastes as its parents. Tastes change and, indeed, the nature of contemporary art is to be fresh and new, but what is 'fresh and new' for the founder might seem 'old hat' to their heirs. Interest in the collection might wither and visits dwindle, while the bills continue to mount up.

'Not thinking this stuff through seems an act of total hubris. You create this monster, you say to your kids don't worry and then you go and die and they are stuck with overheads, a collection they don't like and a set of public responsibilities,' comments cultural consultant Adrian Ellis.[3] In many instances the quality of the collection means that future generations will enjoy it and it will remain relevant as a 'time capsule' of a certain period, place or person. Museums founded on collections such as those of Isabella Stewart Gardner, Albert Barnes, Sir John Soane or the Wallace Collection do not need to be updated, nor indeed does the Villa Panza, Count Giuseppe Panza di Biumo's collection of Minimalist American art in Varese, Italy.[4]

In the case of a few lauded collections, heirs might be proud to be associated with their parents' work, but often this is not the case. Successors rarely have the same taste and the danger is that they might be tempted to disperse the collection, so destroying their parents' legacy. Or they might sell some of the holdings to sustain the rest. But here's the rub – the works of art that attract the public and define the collection are generally the ones that make the most money. The lesser material, even if significant to the assemblage, tends to have a much lower resale value.

After the death of the Barcelona collector Josep Suñol in late 2019, some of the highlights of his private museum – single works by Alexander Calder, Manolo Millares, Antoni Tàpies and Antonio Saura – went for sale at Christie's, raising almost £6 million.[5] Stripping out the jewels may have saved the small museum, but its interest for visitors will surely be diminished, while the local press lamented that the loss of such significant works was a 'hecatomb', impoverishing the city's cultural offer.[6]

The question arises of who will take over on the founder's death. They were the ones who sustained the project financially, drove it forward and whose vision and taste made it what it was. A salaried curator/director might already be in place, supported by a board, although in many cases that board consists of the owner's family. But will this person have the same vision and drive, and will the terms of the endowment allow continuing acquisitions? It is too early to say what will happen when the founders of this century's crop of private museums pass on; the Suñol example cited above is one of the few recent cases. However, the past has seen some near-death experiences, notably the Menil Collection in Houston, which was only made secure after an injection of $240 million from Dominique de Menil's estate.[7]

While not everyone applauds the choices made for Eli Broad's museum in Los Angeles – see Chapter 3 – one thing stands out: the real estate magnate was extraordinarily generous in his home city, supporting manifold cultural venues. And he endowed his foundation with $200 million, to ensure its survival beyond his demise, which happened in 2021. However, is that enough? According to Georgina Walker, Director Emeritus John Walsh believes the sum is insufficient to continue to acquire new works comparable with those already in the museum.[8] But at least, unlike some other private museums, it does have an endowment – many have none.

Here today, gone tomorrow . . .

The number of private museums that have already closed is startling and the COVID-19 pandemic might trigger more closures. At the time of writing, it is impossible to say how many might be affected, although museum associations have already warned that the impact will be severe. But even before the pandemic, closures were more frequent than is often realised. Probably the highest profile instance in recent years is that of the much-trumpeted Marciano Art Foundation in Los Angeles. This was established and funded by brothers Paul and Maurice Marciano, half of the original quartet behind the $1.1 billion Guess brand.

The brothers had converted a former Masonic temple into a showcase for their hefty, 1500-strong collection of art-market favourites, largely built up during a seven-year buying spree. After a splashy opening in the vast building – which cost $8 million – the museum snapped shut after only two and a half years. The brothers blamed poor attendance, but staff cited labour disputes.[9] Part of the building has now been leased to the commercial gallery Gagosian.

While the Marciano closure was the most spectacular, many other private museums are no more: for example, the Main, a non-collecting, non-profit contemporary space also in Los Angeles, which closed in 2019. It had opened three years before with big ambitions, the brainchild of local developers Tom Gilmore and Jerri Perrone. Gilmore had long been combining art with real estate projects, notably by leasing storefronts in buildings he owned to galleries. According to *Artnet,* he originally used a $27.5 million loan – backed by a federal redevelopment project – to bring in art projects, gentrify neighbourhoods and reap the rewards. 'Once a neighbourhood has high-end restaurants, lofts, and galleries, few things underscore its cultural significance better than a new contemporary art museum,' wrote *Artnet.*[10] There was apparently a mismatch between the founder's vision and that of the staff he hired; it seems his hopes of boosting the gentrification of the area ran counter to some of the choices made by the curators.

Closures have happened around the world: in Paris, Antoine de Galbert shuttered his much-admired space, La Maison Rouge, in 2018; in London, the Dairy, founded by collector Frank Cohen, lasted just two years, closing in 2014 (but his Manchester space continues). In Toronto, the well-respected Ydessa Hendeles Art Foundation shut its doors in 2012. There has also been a spate of physical spaces that have closed but continued their programming in an 'outreach' mode – examples are the David Roberts Foundation in London, or the Cisneros Fontanals Art Foundation in Miami; both continue to organise exhibitions in other locations, as well as maintaining their commissioning programmes. Indeed, of the 50 museums featured in a smart coffee-table book, *Private Spaces for Contemporary Art*, dating from 2010 and written by the Ukrainian-American museum director Peter Doroshenko, ten have closed or changed their model.

We have seen, then, that most of the cases of defunct private museums come back to the issue of cost. As Ellis notes: 'It's more fun building a museum and opening it than running it. At some point this is about people having fun, but then they and their successors are left with this institution and it can be quite a heavy burden. The successors may not be as motivated as the founders.'[11] A prime example is that of the Corcoran Gallery of Art in Washington DC, one of the US's oldest museums, which closed in 2014 after the board of the financially struggling institution decided it could no longer continue. Another example is the Coninx Museum in Zurich, Switzerland, which had a huge and eclectic collection, from Buddha sculptures to works by Gustav Klimt and Egon Schiele. It closed in 2011 and the collections were put on permanent loan to other institutions.

Or the funding might simply disappear; this was the case with the 6000-strong Essl Collection of Austrian and international art in Klosterneuburg, Austria. When the founder's company bauMax collapsed, so did the museum which it had financed. In the end, part of the collection was sold at auction, and the rest donated to the Albertina Museum in Vienna.

Another reason is disengagement, when the project no longer fulfils the objectives of the founder(s), who may have started out with high ideals but also seeking social and cultural prestige. If this is disappointing – and, in addition, the space is proving a major drain on resources – the founder has a double reason to pull the plug. An example might be the Louise Blouin Foundation's London base, a former coachworks factory in the west of the city. Beautifully restored and inaugurated in 2006, the 3200 m^2 space was lit up at night by a permanent James Turrell light installation. But the owner, the eccentric Louise Blouin, became disengaged and the space was sold in 2019, with the Turrell installation gone long before.

The pressures of running an art space can also have an impact. Ziba Ardalan created Parasol Unit in London's East End but, after 16 years, decided to close it in 2020. Holding four exhibitions a year, supporting young artists and putting them on the map, Parasol received considerable acclaim for its forward-thinking programme. Among those shown there were Michaël Borremans, Yang Fudong, Y.Z. Kami, Charles Avery, Bharti Kher, David Claerbout, Tschabalala Self and Martin Puryear.

Ardalan initially funded the space along with her Swiss husband, although because of its education programme and non-profit status, it received public funding including grants from the Arts Council and the Henry Moore Foundation. Asked why she decided to close, Ardalan said:

> Firstly, the art world had changed dramatically since I opened the space in 2004. Secondly, space-wise, I had done almost everything I could have done and it is natural that after so many years one needs to move on. And finally, the excessively hot art market in the pre-Covid time, meant younger staff in London were feeling they needed to move rather fast from one job to another in order to gain experience. This was demanding from management point of view and made it hard to build up an organisation properly.[12]

Generational change was partly an issue here, as was the case with the much-admired Cass Sculpture Foundation in Goodwood, Sussex, in the south of England, where pressing financial problems compounded by the ages of the founders – 92 and 94 – led to a sudden shut-down in 2019.[13]

Finally, there may be actual cases of wrongdoing which sink a project. 'Art-washing' – using art to burnish a dodgy past – has been behind a few projects which have bitten the dust. In Moscow, owners of two private museums have become fugitives from justice. The Institute of Russian Realist Art was locked down after its founders fled abroad to avoid charges of embezzlement;[14] the other, the Museum of Russian Impressionism, was still functioning at the time of writing, although its founder, billionaire Boris Mints, had fled Russia.[15]

Another scandal struck a major Portuguese collector, José Berardo – once dubbed the 'Portuguese Saatchi'. The mining entrepreneur had amassed a collection of over 900 works including pieces by Joan Miró, Piet Mondrian, Francis Bacon and Gerhard Richter, and the group was put on display in 2006 in a public gallery – the Centro Cultural de Belém in Lisbon – as part of a private-public partnership with the Portuguese government. But it turned out that Berardo had been pledging the art as collateral to three banks, to borrow a total of almost €1 billion; the banks filed lawsuits to recover the debt.[16] Despite this, Berardo opened a second museum – of Art Nouveau and Art Deco objects – in the centre of the Portuguese capital in April 2021. It transpired that the protocol signed by Berardo and the Portuguese state meant that the works of art in his first museum could not be seized, since they belonged to a foundation, not to Berardo. In June 2021, Berardo was arrested in Portugal over allegations of being involved in a multimillion-dollar fraud plot;[17] at the time of writing, the museum was still open.

Finally, there is the strange fate of the two Pinacothèque museums – one in Paris, the other in Singapore. Founded by the art historian and Modigliani specialist Marc Restellini, the Paris Pinacothèque had a small and eclectic collection mainly lent by private collectors, but its main focus was curated shows of loaned works. Well placed on the prestigious Place de la Madeleine, the Pinacothèque hosted exhibitions between 2007 and 2015, some with catch-all titles that tended to trumpet a big name (*Giacometti and the Etruscans*, 2011, or *Jackson Pollock and Shamanism*, 2008). However, 'It was a really dreadful place, very poorly lit, with a few third-rate works by well-known artists,' comments the French journalist Roxana Azimi.[18]

In 2015 Restellini opened a second outlet in Singapore in Fort Canning, a colonial-era building which was revamped into a cultural centre with shops and restaurants as well as the museum. This was a partnership between Restellini, the Singapore Diamond Exchange chairman Alain Vandenborre, the 'freeport king' Yves Bouvier and an investment company. The Singapore Tourist Board also put in some money, and the space opened with a show of Old Masters and early

20th-century works – from Botticelli to Picasso – 'on loan from private collectors around the world', according to the press release.

The Parisian Pinacothèque went into receivership in 2015, owing €2 million. Rental on the building, owned by the French bank Crédit Agricole, had not been paid for two years. At the time, according to Restellini, a sharp drop in attendance numbers following terrorist attacks in Paris was to blame, putting the Pinacothèque into the red.[19] A few months later, the Singapore branch also closed very suddenly, leaving unpaid debts of about SG$900,000 (about £510,000).[20] Again, poor attendance figures were given as a reason. Restellini had claimed that the two operations were financed separately, but the timing of the closure corresponded with the developing bitter legal battle between the investor Yves Bouvier and his former client Dmitry Rybolovlev; the previous year a Singapore court had temporarily frozen Bouvier's worldwide assets.[21]

Ultimately, many of these failures demonstrate the fragility of spaces that rely on a single founder, whose motivations and financial stability may change, or who may not have realised the difficulties inherent in establishing their own art space.

Conclusion

The question now is where will private museums be in ten, 20 or even 50 years' time? And indeed, where will public institutions be over that same time frame? How will both public and private art spaces evolve, how will they fit into the art ecology of the future, and how will they integrate with the public sector – or will they do so at all?

As we have seen, some private museums will die while new ones are created; others will become absorbed into the public sphere through partnerships, as indeed happened in the 19th century. The public-private model is already widespread in Germany, where it has enabled cities to show collections they could not otherwise afford and greatly enriched their cultural offering. When this generation of private museum founders dies out, will their successors increasingly turn to the state to take on the burden, or will they simply liquidate the holdings? One eminent London-based museum director told me: 'I think there will be a lot of art offered to us as the founders pass on . . . but we won't want much of it.'[1]

There are good reasons for this – in many countries, once a work is acquired for a public institution, it can never leave; and longer-term, what will institutions do with all that art? Because, make no mistake, currently there is tremendous overproduction of art, forcing anyone wanting to present a complete picture of today's contemporary creation, in all its diversity, to constantly acquire the latest examples. But the fashionable fades rapidly and, to remain relevant, collections of contemporary art must renew themselves continually. This is where the private sector has an important role to play, with its rapid decision-making and ability to deaccession just as speedily when a trend, name or practice is no longer significant. Mistakes can be made, obviously, but private owners' ability to 'refine' their collections is a tremendous plus.

By the same token, there are dangers. For a start, the wealth and sway of private collectors risk rewriting art history as a function of their acquisitions. This could either be if they have a shiny museum to showcase them in or are able to influence publicly funded museums for which they are donors or trustees. Art market specialist Alain Quemin cites the example of François Pinault: '[He] has been criticized as an example of the use of private money shaping the public sphere of arts through financing and loan of works ... This also includes influence over the choice of artists.'[2] And Quemin particularly notes the cases of Martial Raysse and Jeff Koons – artists whom Pinault collects – who both had solo exhibitions at the Centre Pompidou in Paris, despite museum curators having reservations about the quality and type of the work displayed: post-1960s work for Raysse, painting for Koons. 'It would be wrong to blame the president of Centre Pompidou,' continues Quemin delicately. 'When acquisitions budgets for contemporary art are particularly low ... the persons who are in charge of museums are strongly inclined – and often compelled – to maintain good relations with prominent collectors and galleries.'

Then there is the thorny problem of price and the 21st-century obsession with money. Do Jeff Koons's fabulous prices make him the most significant contemporary artist in the world, just because of the record $91.1 million given in 2019 for his 1986 *Rabbit*?[3] Koons's work features in The Broad in Los Angeles, in the Victor Pinchuk and the Pinault collections, while a group show in the New Museum in New York was curated by Koons and featured an extensive selection of his works from collector Dakis Joannou's collection.[4] Is this a way of moulding the cultural discourse of today?

Another criticism levelled at many private collections is that they tend to concentrate on just a few, market-friendly names, again skewing the discourse. Indeed, curator and museum director Chris Dercon has written: 'Often these private collections look much the same. With some exceptions, today's private museums for contemporary art are clones.'[5] It could be argued that traditional museums do the same thing, all showing, for example, Matisse, Picasso or Braque – but their choices have had the advantage of the passing of time, allowing them to reach a consensus about which artists are relevant and significant in the arc of art history.

Private owners' collections are ultimately representative of a single, very wealthy individual's taste, sometimes coupled with that of their advisors. This is not necessarily a bad thing, as museums such as Sir John Soane's Museum or the Frick Collection demonstrate, but such collections are the antithesis of the mission of public museums. A private museum will generally show what the owner bought and liked, reflecting that singular point of view. A public museum is more inclusive and polyphonic, with curators from different fields presenting a far more diverse range of creation, to give the public a broader view of art history and of the place of cultural artefacts within society.

More worryingly, unlike in the past when many private collectors ultimately donated to public institutions, in today's world there is a real likelihood that works put into a private museum may never enrich the public sector. Their ownership and display will be subject to the whims of their owners – or, on their death, to those of their successors, as we saw in Chapter 6.

In Chapter 2, Sir Mark Jones – a former director of the Victoria and Albert Museum – told me: 'You'd be pretty mad to give [your collection] to the British Museum or the Victoria and Albert.' As András Szántó asks: 'Why didn't public institutions become so sexy, so innovative, so indispensable, so avant-garde – not just in the eyes of a narrow art audience but for society at large – that any forward-looking, enterprising benefactor would consider him or herself to be a fool to not want to stand under that umbrella?"[6]

The shock of the 2020–21 pandemic and the other pressures outlined in the Introduction are bringing far-reaching changes to publicly funded museums. They are being forced to become more inclusive, more socially committed, to engage wider audiences and to become more diverse, both in the choices of what they exhibit and in their staffing. Private museums, relying as they do on their founders' choices, are less subject to these challenges. However, the sheer number showing contemporary art, and dependent for survival on their founders and successors, makes me wonder how many will be sustained into the future. I suspect that the best – the best-funded, with the smartest buildings, the most interesting collections – will survive but that many will not last long beyond the death of their founders.

Ultimately, both public and private museums should have the same goals – to advance visual arts, contribute to society, enrich the community and benefit the public. Some of the unease we feel about private museums, however, comes from our grudging appreciation of what they do – coupled with distrust of their motives – and the way they sometimes highlight the glaring wealth inequality of our time. But this inequality has also given us some wonderful things. When the Fondation Louis Vuitton treats Parisian collectors with a sensational show from the Morozov collection; or the Museum of Contemporary Art Africa in Cape Town gives African creators a platform they never had before; when Eli Broad endowed his space with $200 million to ensure its survival; or the Muzeum Susch puts a tiny Swiss village on the map with a display of Polish artists; or the Fondazione Sandretto Re Rebaudengo offers Turin the chance to see talented young names . . . these are shining examples and powerful reasons to celebrate private museums in all their diversity.

Notes

Introduction

1 Originally used to refer to the Guggenheim Museum Bilbao in north-west Spain.

2 Paul Vallely, *Philanthropy: From Aristotle to Zuckerberg* (Bloomsbury, London, 2020), p.149.

3 This and subsequent quotes from András Szántó, interview with the author, November 2019.

4 Speaker did not want to be identified.

5 This and subsequent quotes from Alain Quemin, interview with the author, January 2020.

6 Email from Centre Pompidou, Paris, 17 February 2020.

7 Scheduled to run from 21 May to October 2021.

8 22 October 2016 to 5 March 2017; according to *The Art Newspaper*'s annual attendance survey, 2018.

9 3 October to 21 January 2019.

10 Interview with the author, July 2019, speaker did not wish to be identified.

1: What is a Private Museum?

1 Georgina S. Walker, *The Private Collector's Museum: Public Good versus Private Gain* (Routledge, Oxford, 2019), p.1.

2 This and subsequent quotes from Maxwell Anderson, interview with the author, December 2019. For an explanation of 501(c)(3) status, see Chapter 3.

3 Email from Mireia Azuara of CIMAM, 24 January 2020.

4 Interview with the author, May 2019.

5 https://www.theleidencollection.com/

6 https://hillartfoundation.org/

7 Walker, p.44.

8 Interview with the author via Zoom, September 2020.

9 https://www.forbes.com/profile/francois-pinault/?sh=5313ed434d20

10 Gareth Harris, 'Pinault pulls the plug on Paris Museum, *The Art Newspaper*, 31 May 2001, https://www.theartnewspaper.com/archive/pinault-pulls-the-plug-on-paris-museum.

11 This and subsequent quotes from Sébastien Montabonel, interview with the author, July 2019.

12 Emmanuel Lévy, 'Les comptes fantastiques de la fondation Louis Vuitton', *Marianne*, 13 May 2017, https://www.marianne.net/societe/les-comptes-fantastiques-de-la-fondation-louis-vuitton.

13 Suzanne Kapner, 'Pinault wins long battle to control Gucci Group, *New York Times*, 11 September 2001, https://www.nytimes.com/2001/09/11/business/pinault-wins-long-battle-to-control-gucci-group.html.

14 31 August 2019 to 12 January 2020.

15 Interview with the author, August 2019.

16 Email to the author from K11 spokesperson, 1 June 2020.

17 Email to the author from Tony Salamé, 21 September 2020.

18 Quoted in Georgina Adam, 'Why shopping malls are making space for high-end art', *The Art Newspaper*, 31 March 2016, https://www.theartnewspaper.com/news/why-shopping-malls-are-making-space-for-high-end-art.

19 Maximilíano Durón, 'Bernardo Paz, Top Brazilian Art Collector and Founder of Inhotim, Cleared of Money Laundering Charges', *Artnews*, 27 February 2020, https://www.artnews.com/art-news/news/collector-bernardo-paz-criminal-charges-cleared-1202679199/.

2: The Founders and their Motivations

1 This and subsequent quotes from Sir Mark Jones, interview with the author, June 2019.

2 Interview with the author, July 2019.

3 *Private Art Museum Report*, edited by Larry's List Ltd. and AMMA, Vienna, January 2016.

4 Andrew Russeth, '"Art Saved Our Marriage": Mera and Don Rubell Toast 50 Years Together, in São Paulo', *Artnews*, 10 April 2015, https://www.artnews.com/art-news/news/art-saved-our-marriage-mera-and-don-rubell-toast-50-years-together-in-sao-paulo-3919/.

5 Anand Giridharadas, *Winners Take All: The Elite Charade of Changing the World* (Allen Lane, London, 2019), p.157.
6 This and subsequent quotes from Adrian Ellis, interview with the author, November 2019.
7 Nina Siegal, 'Maja Hoffmann Fights to Build Her Cultural Capital in Arles, France', *The New York Times*, 5 October 2018, https://www.nytimes.com/2018/10/05/arts/design/arles-france-maja-hoffmann.html.
8 Christine Coste, 'François Hébel quitte Arles', *Le Journal des Arts*, 19 November 2013, https://www.lejournaldesarts.fr/actualites/francois-hebel-quitte-arles-119929.
9 John Gapper, 'Billionaires have franchised the modern art museum', *Financial Times*, 8 August 2018, https://www.ft.com/content/af4638ee-9a40-11e8-ab77-f854c65a4465.
10 According to a source who has asked not to be identified, conversation with the author, July 2019.
11 https://www.forbes.com/billionaires/
12 'Elon Musk becomes world's richest person as wealth tops $185bn', *BBC News*, 7 January 2021, https://www.bbc.co.uk/news/technology-55578403.
13 *The Savior for Sale*, Zadik Productions, France, 2021.
14 24 October 2019 to 24 February 2020.
15 Anna Brady, 'Botticelli portrait sells for record $92.1m at Sotheby's in New York', *The Art Newspaper*, 28 January 2021, https://www.theartnewspaper.com/news/botticelli-portrait-sells-for-at-sotheby-s-in-new-york.
16 Press release, 6 November 2017, https://www.globalwitness.org/en/press-releases/paradise-papers-expose-flight-risks-posed-anonymous-companies-and-private-us-aircraft/#:~:text=Documents%20obtained%20by%20the%20International%20Consortium%20of%20Investigative,company%20that%20is%20on%20the%20U.S.%20sanctions%20list.
17 Interview with the author, November 2019.
18 Interview with the author, August 2019.
19 Conversation with the author, February 2020.
20 Interview with the author, March 2020.
21 John King, 'Fishers give up on plans for Presidio Art Museum', *Sfgate*, 2 July 2009, https://www.sfgate.com/news/article/Fishers-give-up-on-plan-for-Presidio-art-museum-3225626.php.
22 Conversation with the author, March 2020.
23 Kathy Matheson, 'Judge upholds Barnes Foundation's move to Philly', *6abc news*, 7

October 2011, https://6abc.com/archive/8382143/.

24 Mark Brown, 'Untapped treasure: Wallace collection to start lending artworks', *Guardian*, 24 September 2019, https://www.theguardian.com/artanddesign/2019/sep/24/untapped-treasure-wallace-collection-to-start-lending-artworks.

25 Taylor Dafoe, 'SFMOMA Sold a Rothko for $50 Million to Diversify Its Collection. Here's What They Bought With the Proceeds', *Artnet*, 26 June 2019, https://news.artnet.com/exhibitions/using-funds-deaccessioned-rothko-sfmoma-acquired-11-new-works-address-representational-gaps-permanent-collection-1585570.

26 José da Silva and Martin Bailey, 'British Museum hit hardest by 2020 lockdown among UK's big museums', *The Art Newspaper*, 30 March 2021, https://www.theartnewspaper.com/news/attendance-at-uk-s-flagship-museums-hit-by-covid-19-in-2020.

27 Nancy Kenney, 'AAMD loosens rules for museums that seek to divert income in response to coronavirus crisis', *The Art Newspaper*, 15 April 2020, https://www.theartnewspaper.com/news/aamd-loosens-rules-for-museums-that-seek-to-divert-income-in-response-to-coronavirus-crisis.

28 https://www.christies.com/lot/lot-lucas-cranach-i-lucretia-6281980/?from=searchresults&intObjectID=6281980.

29 Quoted in Georgina S. Walker, *The Private Collector's Museum: Public Good versus Private Gain* (Routledge, Oxford, 2019), p.7.

30 This and subsequent quotes from Mera Rubell, interview with the author, November 2019.

31 This and subsequent quotes from Maxwell Anderson, interview with the author, December 2019.

32 Interview with the author, September 2019.

33 This and subsequent quotes from Rajeeb Samdani, interview with the author, June 2019.

34 Interview with the author, September 2019.

35 This and subsequent quotes from Anita Zabludowicz, interview with the author, May 2019.

36 Kate Brown, '25 Artists Have 'Deauthored' Their Works in the Zabludowicz Collection Because of Its Ties to the Israeli Military', *Artnet*, 27 July 2021, https://news.artnet.com/art-world/zabludowicz-boycott-deauthor-1992711.

37 https://www.delacruzcollection.org/.

38 William Cook, 'The Bilbao effect: How 20 years of Gehry's Guggenheim

transformed the city', *BBC*, 16 October 2017, https://www.bbc.co.uk/programmes/articles/1HL3drXNNWQVq7tpC6pMRsJ/the-bilbao-effect-how-20-years-of-gehrys-guggenheim-transformed-the-city#:~:text=Twenty%20years%20ago%2C%20Bilbao%20was,the%20transformative%20effect%20of%20art. 16 October 2017, *BBC,* 'The Bilbao effect: How 20 years of Gehry's Guggenheim transformed the city', https://www.bbc.co.uk/programmes/articles/1HL3drXNNWQVq7tpC6pMRsJ/the-bilbao-effect-how-20-years-of-gehrys-guggenheim-transformed-the-city.

39 'Tasmania Tourism Statistics', Camperchamp.com, 8 October 2020, https://camperchamp.com.au/statistics/australia/tasmania-tourism/#:~:texthttps://camperchamp.com.au/statistics/australia/tasmania-tourism/#:~:text=Over%20percent203.5%20percent20million%20percent20tourists%20percent20and,July%20percent202018%20percent20and%20percent20June%20percent202019.&text=This%20percent20total%20percent20includes%20percent20300%20percent2C000%20percent20international,billion%20percent20in%20percent20Tasmania%20percent20in%20percent202019.

41 Interview with the author, January 2020.

42 Kate Taylor, 'Controversy surrounds a Christie's Auction', *NY Sun*, 5 March 2007, https://www.nysun.com/arts/controversy-surrounds-a-christies-auction/49749/.

43 Burton B. Fredericksen, *The Burdens of Wealth: Paul Getty and his Museum* (Archway Publishing, Bloomington, 2015), p.2.

3: Financing the Private Museum

1 William Poundstone, 'Main Museum Closes', Lacma On Fire Blog, 15 January 2019, http://lacmaonfire.blogspot.com/2019/01/main-museum-closes.html.

2 Sale at Sotheby's in New York on 28 January 2021.

3 Georgina Adam, 'Billionaire art collector Sheldon Solow's tax-exempt art foundation was infamously inaccessible – now his widow says she will open it to the public', *The Art Newspaper*, 19 November 2020, https://www.theartnewspaper.com/news/sheldon-solow.

4 Michael Shnayerson, 'Inside the Private Museums of Billionaire Art Collectors', *Town and Country*, 16 January 2016, https://www.townandcountrymag.com/leisure/arts-and-culture/a9124/private-museums-of-billionaires/.

5 https://www.causeiq.com/organizations/view_990/205938416/78b153498b24f6a86ffc01a08f99395d.

6 Julia Halperin, 'The Broad, as big as its Founders' Influence', *The Art Newspaper*, 30 September 2015, 'The Broad, as big as its Founders' Influence', https://www.theartnewspaper.com/news/the-broad-as-big-as-its-founders-influence.

7 Costs of the three museums taken from: Frank Peter Jäger, *Old & New: Design Manual for Revitalizing Existing Buildings* (Birkhäuser, Basel, 2010), pp 68–71; https://en.wikipedia.org/wiki/Palazzo_Grassi; https://www.theartnewspaper.com/news/francois-pinault-s-long-awaited-paris-gallery-will-open-next-june.

8 'Under an agreement for the occupation of the public domain concluded with the City of Paris in December 2006, the Fondation Louis Vuitton has a 1 hectare plot of land at its disposal for 55 years, as of 1 January 2007, to set up a building dedicated to art and creation.' Email to author from Fondation Louis Vuitton, 16 February 2020.

9 David Callahan, *The Givers – Wealth, Power and Philanthropy in a New Gilded Age* (First Vintage Books, New York, 2018), p.238.

10 Deborah Vankin, 'Lucas Museum appoints a chief curator and five more women to key roles', *Los Angeles Times*, 9 July 2020, https://www.latimes.com/entertainment-arts/story/2020-07-09/lucas-museum-narrative-art-hiring-curators.

11 Interview with the author, June 2020.

12 Interview with the author, March 2019.

13 Cristina Bechtler and Dora Imhof (eds), *The Private Museum of the Future* (Ringier, Zurich, 2018), p.169.

14 All quotes from Kenny Schachter, interview with the author, November 2020. A spokesperson for Glenstone declined to respond to this comment. Two emails requesting comment from The Broad were not answered.

15 Michael Shnayerson, 'Inside the private museums of billionaire art collectors', *Town and Country*, 16 January 2017, https://www.townandcountrymag.com/leisure/arts-and-culture/a9124/private-museums-of-billionaires/.

16 Paul Vallely, *Philanthropy: From Aristotle to Zuckerberg* (Bloomsbury, London, 2020), p.607.

17 Found at https://projects.propublica.org/nonprofits/.

18 This is the total taxable income remaining after allowable deductions.

19 This and subsequent quotes from Howard Rachofsky, interview with the author, December 2019.

20 https://www.finance.senate.gov/imo/media/doc/Letter%20to%20IRS%20on%20Private%20Museums.pdf

21 Email to author from Diana Wierbicki, 22 February 2021.

22 This and subsequent quotes from Doug Woodham, interview with the author, December 2019.

23 Interview with the author, December 2019.

24 Emmanuelle Lévy, 'Les comptes fantastiques de la fondation Louis Vuitton', *Marianne*, 13 May 2017, https://www.marianne.net/societe/les-comptes-fantastiques-de-la-fondation-louis-vuitton.

25 Nicole Vulser, 'Mécénat: la Cour des comptes critique l'absence de contrôle de l'Etat, *Le Monde*, 28 November 2018, https://www.lemonde.fr/economie/article/2018/11/28/mecenat-la-cour-des-comptes-critique-l-absence-de-controle-de-l-etat_5389770_3234.html.

26 Emmanuel Lévy, 'Fondation Vuitton: Bernard Arnault ou l'art de plumer le contribuable avec un mécénat bidon', *Marianne*, 18 October 2018, https://www.marianne.net/economie/fondation-vuitton-bernard-arnault-ou-l-art-de-plumer-le-contribuable-avec-un-mecenat-bidon. Author's translation.

27 Private Art Museum Report, 2016, p.100.

28 Conversation with the author, June 2020.

29 https://en.unesco.org/news/covid-19-unesco-and-icom-concerned-about-situation-faced-worlds-museums.

30 Julia Jacobs and Zachary Small, 'How Long Can N.Y.C. Museums Survive at 25 Percent Capacity?', *New York Times*, 26 October 2020, https://www.nytimes.com/2020/10/26/arts/design/nyc-museums-covid-capacity.html.

31 https://www.aam-us.org/wp-content/uploads/2020/07/2020_National-Survey-of-COVID19-Impact-on-US-Museums.pdf.

32 Nancy Kenney, 'The Met will not reopen until mid-August at the earliest', *The Art Newspaper*, 19 May 2020, https://www.theartnewspaper.com/news/the-met-will-not-reopen-until-mid-august-at-the-earliest.

33 Kerry A. Dolan, 'Forbes' 35th Annual World's Billionaires List: Facts And Figures 2021', *Forbes*, 6 April 2021, https://www.forbes.com/sites/kerryadolan/2021/04/06/forbes-35th-annual-worlds-billionaires-list-facts-and-figures-2021/?sh=1173eec05e58.

4: The Proliferation of Private Museums in China

1 This and further quotes from Rebecca Wei, interview with the author, June 2020.

2 'Cultural Revolution', *The Economist*, 23 May 2014, https://www.economist.com/books-and-arts/2014/05/23/cultural-revolution.

3 Email to the author, July 2020.

4 Shaun Wang, *Snapshot: Independent, investigative interviews on Chinese contemporary 'Private Museums'* (self-published, Shaun Wang, 2017), p.9.

5 Email to author from Long Museum, 5 February 2021.

6 Communication from Lisa Movius, 1 February 2021.

7 Andrew Goldstein, 'Collector Budi Tek on His "Mission Impossible": To Give China Its First Public Contemporary Art Museum Before He Dies', *Artnet*, 5 February 2019, https://news.artnet.com/art-world/budi-tek-interview-part-1-1455346.

8 Jennifer Wang, 'China Rich List 2020: 68 Newcomers Include The Country's First Vaping Billionaire And 22 Healthcare Fortunes', *Forbes*, 4 November 2020, https://www.forbes.com/sites/jenniferwang/2020/11/04/china-rich-list-2020-68-newcomers-join-the-ranks-as-cutoff-rises-to-155-billion/?sh=1edd8f02644b.

9 Neil Connor, 'Meet the Chinese billionaire behind the record Amedeo Modigliani purchase', *Daily Telegraph*, 10 November 2015, https://www.telegraph.co.uk/news/worldnews/asia/china/11986987/Meet-the-Chinese-billionaire-behind-the-record-Amedeo-Modigliani-purchase.html.

10 Quoted in Georgia McCafferty, 'China's private museums: Icons or empty vanity projects?', *CNN*, 2 December 2016, https://edition.cnn.com/style/article/china-private-art-museums/index.html.

11 Christopher DeWolf, 'Uli Sigg Collection, a window into modern China – and today's Hong Kong', *Zolimacitymag*, 26 February 2016, https://zolimacitymag.com/m-uli-sigg-collection-a-window-into-modern-china-and-todays-hong-kong/.

12 Vivienne Chow, 'Better Days Will Come': Swiss Collector Uli Sigg on Why Even a Less Free Hong Kong Remains the Best Home for His Peerless Chinese Art Collection', *Artnet*, 1 June 2020, https://news.artnet.com/art-world/uli-sigg-interview-1872105.

13 Kanis Leung, 'Chief of Hong Kong's troubled West Kowloon arts hub vows to handle inaugural exhibitions at flagship museum in accordance with national security law', *South China Morning Post*, 23 March 2021, https://www.scmp.com/news/hong-kong/politics/article/3126672/chief-hong-kongs-troubled-west-kowloon-arts-hub-vows-handle.

14 Shaun Wang, 2017, p.37.

15 ibid.

16 ibid, p.39.

17 According to a number of sources who did not want to be identified.

18 Shaun Wang, 2017, p.147.

19 Enid Tsui, 'Guy Ullens "attacked at board meeting" for seeking profit from sale of gallery', *South China Morning Post*, 7 October 2016, https://www.scmp.com/culture/arts-entertainment/article/2026001/guy-ullens-attacked-board-meeting-seeking-profit-sale.

20 This and subsequent quotes from Rebecca Catching, email to the author, 19 December 2019.

21 *Alberto Giacometti Retrospective*, 22 March to 31 July 2016.

22 1 September to 31 December 2015.

23 Gareth Harris, 'Budi Tek reveals landmark deal with Lacma to preserve his collection', *The Art Newspaper*, 29 March 2018, https://www.theartnewspaper.com/news/budi-tek-reveals-landmark-deal-with-lacma-to-preserve-his-collection.

24 Source did not wish to be identified, interview with the author, July 2020.

25 Roxana Azimi, 'Le Centre Pompidou Shanghai doit encore faire ses preuves', *Le Quotidien de l'Art*, 6 November 2020.

5: From Private to Public – Partnerships

1 Cristina Bechtler and Dora Imhof (eds), *The Private Museum of the Future* (JRP Ringier, Geneva, 2018), p.189.

2 Interview with the author, January 2020.

3 Interview with the author, November 2019.

4 Marta Gnyp, *The Shift: Art and the Rise to Power of Contemporary Collectors* (Skira, Milan, 2020), p.229.

5 15 December 2012 to 10 March 2013, https://www.whitechapelgallery.org/exhibitions/collection-sandretto-re-rebaudengo-viral-research/.

6 27 to 29 September 2019, https://www.whitechapelgallery.org/exhibitions/v-a-c-live-this-is-not-a-cinema/.

7 http://www.pacificstandardtime.org/.

8 Georgina S. Walker, *The Private Collector's Museum: Public Good versus Private Gain* (Routledge, Oxford, 2019), p.145.

9 ibid., p.155.

10 Catherine Hickley, 'Berlin museums announce "painful" end to loan of "one of the world's most outstanding contemporary art collections"', *The Art Newspaper*, 24 April 2020, https://www.theartnewspaper.com/news/berlin-museums-announce-painful-end-to-flick-collection-loan.

11 'Charles Saatchi gallery deal hits setback', *BBC News*, 6 September 2010, https://www.bbc.co.uk/news/entertainment-arts-11205457.

12 2 November 2019 to 17 March 2020.

13 2 November 2014 to 3 May 2015.

14 Emma Beatty, 'Top German collector disappoints museums by selling loans. Hans Grothe has sold 700 works to Wella hair-care billionaires for E50 million', *The Art Newspaper*, 17 July 2019, https://www.theartnewspaper.com/archive/top-german-collector-disappoints-museums-by-selling-loans.

15 This information and subsequent quotes from Howard Rachofsky, interview with the author, December 2019.

16 *Fast Forward: Contemporary Collections for the Dallas Museum of Art* (Dallas Museum of Art, 2007).

6: Legacy, Sustainability and Why Private Museums Sometimes Die

1 Interview with the author, June 2019.

2 Interview with the author, July 2019.

3 This and subsequent quotes, interview with Adrian Ellis, November 2019.

4 This was donated to Italy's equivalent of Britain's National Trust, the Fondo Ambiente Italiano, in 1996.

5 The ONE sale, 10 July 2020, https://www.christies.com/auctions/global-20th-century.

6 Llucià Homs, 'Are they leaving us?', 28 June 2020, https://lluciahoms.cat/lv-208-28-vi-20-3/.

7 Georgina S. Walker, *The Private Collector's Museum: Public Good versus Private Gain* (Routledge, Oxford, 2019), p.234.

8 ibid., p.223.

9 Stacy Perman, 'Inside the Marciano Art Foundation's spectacular shutdown', *New York Times*, 16 February 2020, https://www.latimes.com/entertainment-arts/story/2020-02-16/la-et-cm-marciano-art-foundation-story-behind-the-closure.

10 Catherine Wagley, 'This California Museum Had Big Ambitions – and Then Shuttered. Here's What It Teaches Us About the Perils of Private Museums', *Artnet*, 5 June 2019, https://news.artnet.com/market/what-happened-at-the-main-1564471.

11 Interview with the author, November 2019.

12 Interview with the author, November 2019.

13 Javier Pes, 'One of the UK's Leading Sculpture Parks Is Shutting Down Amid Financial Woes It Attributes to Brexit and Overspending', *Artnet*, 6 November 2019, https://news.artnet.com/art-world/cass-sculpture-close-brexit-1697106.

14 Sophia Kishkovsky, 'Art trove belonging to Russian billionaire fugitive found hidden in village near Moscow', *The Art Newspaper*, 11 November 2019, https://www.theartnewspaper.com/news/russian-billionaire-s-art-found.

15 Sophia Kishkovsky, 'Founder of museum of Russian Impressionism flees for the UK', *The Art Newspaper,* 28 June 2018, https://www.theartnewspaper.com/news/founder-of-museum-of-russian-impressionism-flees-for-the-uk.

16 'Portugal seizes art from businessman who owes almost £1bn', *Guardian*, 30 July 2019, https://www.theguardian.com/world/2019/jul/30/portugal-seizes-art-from-businessman-jose-berardo.

17 Kate Brown 'A Top Portuguese Art Collector and Museum Founder Has Been Arrested Over His Alleged Ties to a Multimillion-Dollar Fraud Scheme', *Artnet*, 30 June 2021, https://news.artnet.com/art-world/joe-berardo-fraud-allegation-1984692#:~:text=Jos%C3%A9%20Berardo%20was%20arrested%20on%20June%2029%20under,opened%20a%20museum%20to%20his%20collection%20in.

18 Interview with the author, November 2020.

19 Emmanuelle Jardonnet, 'La Pinacothèque de Paris ferme ses portes', *Le Monde*, 12 February 2016, https://www.lemonde.fr/arts/article/2016/02/12/en-redressement-judiciaire-la-pinacotheque-de-paris-annonce-sa-fermeture_4864621_1655012.html.

20 Nur Asyiqin Mohamad Salleh and Lee Jian Xuan, 'Firm behind Singapore Pinacotheque de Paris faces two more lawsuits', *Straits Times*, 15 April 2016, https://www.straitstimes.com/lifestyle/arts/firm-behind-singapore-pinacotheque-de-paris-faces-two-more-lawsuits.

21 See Georgina Adam, *Dark Side of the Boom, The Excesses of the Art Market in the 21st Century* (Lund Humphries, London, 2018) for extensive coverage of this dispute.

Conclusion

1 Speaker wished to remain anonymous, conversation with the author, March 2020.

2 All quotes here from Alain Quemin, 'The market and museums: the increasing power of collectors and private galleries in the contemporary art world', *Journal of Visual Art Practice*, 28 September 2020, https://www.tandfonline.com/doi/abs/10.1080/14702029.2020.1804705.

3 Sold at Christie's New York, 15 May 2019.

4 The exhibition was called *Skin Fruit*, 25 March to 6 June 2010.

5 In Cristina Bechtler and Dora Imhof (eds), *The Private Museum of the Future* (JRP Ringier, Zurich, 2018), p.189.

6 Interview with the author, November 2019.

Further Reading

Adam, Georgina, *Dark Side of the Boom, The Excesses of the Art Market in the 21st Century* (Lund Humphries, London, 2018)

Bechtler, Cristina and Imhof, Dora (eds), *The Private Museum of the Future* (JRP Ringier, Zurich, 2018)

Callahan, David, *The Givers – Wealth, Power and Philanthropy in a New Gilded Age* (First Vintage Books, New York, 2018)

De Corral, María and Lane, John R., *Fast Forward, Contemporary Collections for the Dallas Museum of Art,* (Yale University Press, 2007)

Doroshenko, Peter, *Private Spaces for Contemporary Art* (Rispoli, Brussels, 2010)

Fifth BMW Art Guide by Independent Collectors (Hatje Cantz, Berlin, 2018)

Fredericksen, Burton B., *The Burdens of Wealth: Paul Getty and his Museum* (Archway Publishing, Bloomington, 2015)

Giridharadas, Anand, *Winners Take All: The Elite Charade of Changing the World* (Allen Lane, London, 2019)

Gnyp, Marta, *The Shift: Art and the Rise to Power of Contemporary Collectors* (Skira, Milan, 2020)

Grenier, Catherine, *La Fin des Musées?* (Regard, Paris, 2013)

Jacobson, Clare, *New Museums in China* (Princeton Architectural Press, 2014)

Kirk, Alex E., 'The Billionaire's Treasure Trove: A Call to Reform Private Art Museums and the Private Benefit Doctrine, *Fordham Intell. Prop. Media & Ent. L.J.* vol.27, no.4, 2017, https://ir.lawnet.fordham.edu/iplj/vol27/iss4/4

Lord, Gail (ed.), *Museum Development in China, Understanding the Building Boom* (Rowman and Littlefield, Lanham, MA, 2019)

McClellan, Andrew, *The Art Museum from Boullée to Bilbao* (University of California Press, Berkeley, 2008)

Montabonel, Sébastian, *Art Institutions of the 21st Century* (report: Alaska Editions, London 2016)

Private Art Museum Report, (edited by Larry's List Ltd. and AMMA, Modern Arts Publishing, Vienna, 2016)

Saumarez Smith, Charles, *The Art Museum in Modern Times* (Thames and Hudson, London, 2021)

Szántó, András, *The Future of the Museum, 28 Dialogues* (Hatje Cantz, Berlin, 2020)

Vallely, Paul, *Philanthropy: From Aristotle to Zuckerberg* (Bloomsbury, London, 2020)

Walker, Georgina S., *The Private Collector's Museum: Public Good versus Private Gain* (Routledge, Oxford, 2019)

Walsh, David, *A Bone of Fact* (Picador, Sydney, 2014)

Wang, Shaun, *Snapshot: Independent, investigative interviews on Chinese contemporary 'Private Museums'* (self-published, Shaun Wang, 2017)

Index